Martin Luther's Friends

for
Pauline

Martin Luther's Friends

Noel C. LeRoque

PROVIDENCE HOUSE PUBLISHERS
Franklin, Tennessee

Printed in the United States of America

01   00   99   98   97   5   4   3   2   1

Library of Congress Catalog Card Number: 97–65628

ISBN: 1–57736–022–2

The author gratefully acknowledges the following source as a guide to the spelling of names in this volume: *Martin Luther*, by Martin Brecht, 3 vols. (Fortress Press, 1990).

Cover by Bozeman Design. Cover illustration of Martin Luther (center) with (left to right) Philipp Melanchthon, Johannes Bugenhagen, and Caspar Cruciger. Original lithograph from the collection of Concordia Historical Institute, St. Louis, Missouri.

PROVIDENCE HOUSE PUBLISHERS
238 Seaboard Lane • Franklin, Tennessee 37067
800-321-5692

Contents

Preface

No one can write about Martin Luther and the German Reformation without giving hostages to fortune. One is indeed "splashing at a ten-league canvas with a brush of comet's hair." Scores of books have been published, most of them rather naturally in Germany (and in German), but many of them in other lands and other languages. Every facet of Luther's life has been examined in minute detail, every reasonable approach to the historical facts, as well as how they became facts, has been dissected, pro and con. The setting has been analyzed in historical, economic, social, political, and religious terms. Luther has been given all the credit for one of the great upheavals of history—and everything has been explained in terms that make him only a bit player who happened on the scene at just the right time.

The five hundredth anniversary of the birth of the Reformer, celebrated throughout the world in 1983, reminded us of all this. Books, monographs, newspaper stories, magazine articles, and community celebrations, if anything, added to his stature and certainly made a whole modern generation aware of him and his importance to our life. While *Time* magazine could have been expected, along with *Newsweek* and other such journals, to pay their respects to Luther and his impact on history, some found it rather unexpected that one of the best interpretations of his life and work came in *National Geographic*!

In all of this, however, the plethora of material on Luther developed over the 450 or so years since his death, and brought into focus in 1983 and since, very little has been made available about the friends of Martin Luther. It is as though he operated in a kind of social vacuum. There have been some biographical and other materials published about the close friends of the Friar of Wittenberg, but they are almost entirely in German, have been limited in out-put, and are largely from another time, and apparently now largely out of print. Philipp Melanchthon, of course, has received his share of attention, but generally as a theologian—not as being a close friend of Luther.

But Luther was sociable, friendly (as witness the collection and publication of his "Table Talk"), and dependent upon his friends for understanding, morale-building support, and shoulders to lean on and cry on. They were personal friends and family friends. Some began as friends and followers but found reason in events and their minds to part company. We are here concerned with those who stayed by, no matter what. Justus Jonas rode in the rude cart with him to the Diet of Worms and preached at the service at his death. Melanchthon, John Bugenhagen, and George Spalatin were with Luther at every point, including public as well as familial relationships. The Elector Frederick, and his brother and nephew Electors, never wavered in their support—in spite of questions raised by political and economic considerations. Johann Staupitz nurtured

Luther, maintaining an affection for him in spite of the widening chasm between his protégé and the church.

Our effort here is to give some form and substance to such friends of Luther, not diminishing others, but recognizing their special closeness to him. We are not attempting to evaluate events, to develop theological interpretations, to second-guess the decisions and actions of Luther—only to use the historical records, especially his correspondence—to give a measure of life to these friends. Our thesis is that they were close to Luther and so of importance to him at every significant experience of his life. They have been neglected too long!

There are no footnotes. The text may suggest that I have covered the literature in English, which was my intention. A good share of the literature on Luther and the Reformation in Germany has been out of print for a long time, making necessary much scouring of libraries. So far as I know, there are no English volumes on any but Melanchthon and Kate von Bora. This has meant that, basically, one is reduced to a pastiche of sentences and paragraphs, peripheral notations, material that is frequently unrelated to our purposes.

Most valuable are the volumes on Luther's correspondence, with H. P. Smith and C. F. Jacobs's two volumes leading the way. Tappert's *Luther: Letters of Spiritual Counsel* helped in our effort to humanize character. Durant, in his volume on *The Reformation* put things best in historical perspective. Roland Bainton probably did more than any other to popularize Luther and the Reformation. He used endnotes, rather than footnotes—I would guess in the interest of readability. I found Boehmer's *Road to Reformation—Martin Luther to the Year 1521* a most stimulating study.

My preference in the matter of general Reformation books is the four volumes by James Mackinnon. (In a used-book store in

San Francisco I found a volume by D'Aubigne, published in Switzerland a hundred and fifty years ago, one of a several volume set, that had more of a spread of useful information than in any other book I used. There was also more unusable material, which made for a lot of digging! Either a number of scholars read D'Aubigne or else he preceded them in the study of earlier texts, for a number of them cited the same materials that he had used.)

Though there are none of the trappings of scholarship—i.e., footnotes, the reader may be assured that all quotations, historical references, and time relationships are quite correct. The quotes are from sources long out of copyright problems, and the historical materials are in proper order. There is a redundancy in the use of some of the historical references. This is a result of dealing with each individual as an individual. That is, there was no effort to write a new history of the German Reformation, fitting the individuals in as the history progressed. Rather, our effort was to see these as individual persons, reacting to essentially the same historical milieu.

My thanks are due to daughter, Therese, and granddaughter, Selma, who spent more hours than I had any right to claim in getting this ready for publication. The responsibility is solely mine for any errors of research, judgment, misuse of material, or errors in historical understanding.

And, let us not forget Pauline, my patient, long-suffering wife, who encouraged me to write, and will, I think, be happy with the result.

CHAPTER 1

Introduction

A sure way to refresh one's memory of the wide-ranging effectiveness of the German Protestant Reformation is to walk around and through the Luther Denkmal, the monument to Martin Luther in Worms, Germany. This thriving Rhine-side city has many reminders of the stocky monk who had so much influence on the beliefs, thoughts, and language of countless persons. His theology still echoes from pulpits around the world. His thought on politics and economics and social systems, while superseded by fresh generations of challenge and decision, was crucial for his own time. His importance in the developing language of his own people, through his translations of Scripture, cannot be calculated.

The monument represents these considerations in very personal terms. Luther stands, the central figure, surrounded by some of the men who influenced his thought by their day-to-day involvement in the Reformation and by carrying the message from community to community and nation to nation.

Luther's patron-protector, Frederick the Wise, is there. Philipp Melanchthon is there, as are John Huss and John Wycliffe. Gerolamo Savanarola and Peter Waldus are there.

To be sure, some of them were the "morning stars" of the Reformation, coming on the scene before Luther's time. Bugenhagen, Cruciger, Spalatin, Amsdorf, Staupitz are not included as part of the monument. Perhaps they should be, but nevertheless it is apparent that Luther was not alone when he boldly proclaimed, "Here I stand . . ." Even at this rather early stage in the movement toward reformation, there were friends and colleagues who were learning to know and to understand and to believe in him. The monument says this. And more.

Around the base of the monument are inscribed the names of the cities and towns that were first receptive to the preaching of the gospel. Lords, barons, dukes, landgraves, knights—and common people—opened their hearts and minds to Luther's unheard-of proposal that the true believer could have ready access to the truth of the Book and the heart of God. To be allowed to think for themselves was such heady stuff that excesses occurred. In Wittenberg it was the true believers who smashed the statues of the saints and burned their pictures in the excitement of the immense changes overtaking them.

Everyday, run-of-the-mill people became followers of Luther. His appearances and public utterances drew crowds; his classes were full; his Table Talk became important enough to record; his writings were eagerly read by thousands.

Central to his work, and its success, was a small group of trusted friends and colleagues. Evidently he had "gifts" (charisma) that drew others to him, in spite of his sometimes abrasive personality. His blunt approach did not alienate him from Philipp Melanchthon, however, who was much more concerned than Luther about theological niceties. His complete disregard for personal danger at the hands of kings and popes did not unnerve such as Justus Jonas, who very early positioned himself alongside Luther on the long walk to Worms, and throughout the threatened consequences. His stubbornly wrong response to the Landgrave of Hesse, in the matter of his marriage and bigamy, was supported by Jonas, Melanchthon, and Bugenhagen, all of whom knew better. His crudities did not keep him from being domesticated by his wife, Katherine von Bora, and becoming something of a model husband and father. Quite obviously, people liked him and trusted him.

The creators of the monument included Huss, Wycliffe, Waldus, and Savanarola with the Reformer. They were intellectual and faith friends of Luther. He was prescient enough to follow their beckoning and because of them to plow his own furrow. Denunciation of them by the Church as heretics did not keep him from examining their proposals; and fear of being denounced himself did not keep him from listening to these voices heralding bold theses. These men, although not included here as "friends" of the Friar of Wittenberg, are mentioned to remind us of their important relationship to Luther. Without them, there very likely would have been no Lutheran Reformation; they were the spark that ignited the fire.

Johannes Reuchlin anchors one corner of the monument; this is somewhat surprising, for there are not many references to him in Reformation literature. The great-uncle of Philipp Melanchthon, Reuchlin was a renowned scholar who accepted many of the basic reformation postulates, as did Erasmus of Rotterdam. They were scholar-friends and shared many studies of Scripture and theology that became increasingly important to Luther. Reuchlin recommended Melanchthon to the faculty at Wittenberg and thus had a hand in bringing him and Luther together. He himself, however, was cautious about full acceptance of Lutheran doctrine, though he remained open-minded and tolerant.

Regal, seated figures of women on the monument represent cities where Reformation ideas first were expressed and which had special relationship to Luther: Speier, where German nobles "protested" and gave a name to Protestantism; Augsburg, where Luther faced the Church down in an early confrontation; and Magdeburg, which became a stronghold of evangelicalism in the north.

The monument is impressive and brings to life what history books tell us. There is one facet of Luther's life that is only hinted at: the personal life and relationships of the Reformer. You see this in the figures of Frederick the Wise and Melanchthon who were close to Luther—as personal friend, in the case of Melanchthon, and mentor and supporter in the case of the Elector Frederick.

Some day-in-and-day-out colleagues and personal friends of Luther also greatly influenced his thought and actions and, ultimately, the outcome of the Reformation. They sat where he sat, rejoiced when he rejoiced, wept when he wept. They lived as neighbors; their wives exchanged recipes; their children played together; they could go into each others' houses without knocking. They were close.

These men lived and worked in Luther's shadow, but the way they lived and worked was important in making him great. They were men of substance in their own right, widely known and appreciated, but they were so devoted to Luther that they would not have been offended to be known as "hewers of wood and drawers of water" for him. In addition to Melanchthon, Jonas, Amsdorf, Spalatin, Bugenhagen, Katherine von Bora, Frederick the Elector, and John von Staupitz all have a claim as Luther's friends.

The monument to Martin Luther in Worms, Germany.

I can, perhaps, be taken to task for not demonstrating, with appropriately detailed scholarly research, the specific instances in which friends played a part in Luther's stance and actions at decisive points in his leadership role. In his correspondence, Luther gives credit to Staupitz for his embarking on the "road to reformation," and for continued support and friendship. When Luther was confronting Cajetan in Augsburg, in 1518, Staupitz stood with the rebellious monk, enduring the condemnation of many ecclesiastical superiors. Luther then, and often later, recognized that in Staupitz one could see the precursor and source of his theological and philosophical viewpoints.

Jonas and Amsdorf were with Luther at Worms, not only cheering him on, but sharing the views he expounded. When the roll is called at every point of decision and action in which Luther was involved, they, as well as Melanchthon and Bugenhagen, were "present and accounted for." They not only cooperated with the Reformer in establishing the reforms, they shared in the determination of the nature of the reforms and the need for them. Luther's translation of the Bible owed much to the informal "Bible club" which he established with these friends and a few others, in which the work was carried on as a kind of group project.

The importance of Katherine and the Elector Frederick in Luther's life and work is suggested by one writer: Luther would have died much earlier without the care of his wife, and he could not have continued his zealous enterprise without the protective shield of Frederick. How else could a "lone monk"—his own description—stand against the condemnation of Rome, the coercion of many in authority, a personal journey fraught with recurring illness, and the conviction that political forces would surely make a martyr of him, especially as he lived under the continuing threat of the Edict of Worms.

It is strange that these individuals who were so crucial for the Reformation in Germany have been so neglected by recorders of history. In trying to shed some light on Luther's close friends, we see how very important they were to making him the public figure that he was. That can best be done by seeing them as he saw them.

I have made no effort to write another history of the Reformation, leaving that for the experts. Rather, I have tried to bring individuals to life—without tying them or events to a chronological sequence—by focusing on relationships and intellectual and emotional concerns. This approach puts Luther's friends into the center of events, and moves them out of the shadow of the great Reformer.

CHAPTER 2

The Friar of Wittenberg

hen Martin Luther, Friar of Wittenberg, stood before the Emperor and the princes at the Diet of Worms, the experience was a lonely one even though a number of friends, old and new, had accompanied him there. They were "with him" in the sense of giving moral and physical support. They not only wished him well, they were willing to rally to whatever cause he espoused. From time to time evidence would come of their willingness to die for him and his proposals. Some of them became not only followers, with what that brought in the way of companionship and close acquaintance, but dear friends as well. Yet in this moment Luther was alone.

The impression one gets when scanning the historical picture is one of severity of personal discipline on the part of the young monk which would lead to the exclusion of normal human relationships. Commonly we remember the "Here I stand . . ." image of Luther, or the flagellations of the monk, or the personal diatribes and invectives of feuds with the Church and its leaders. All of these images are of a man by himself. And, at least on some occasions, Luther himself writes and speaks as though he is misunderstood even by his best friends and is alone in the midst of them.

Nevertheless, while recognizing the essentially lonely nature of the experiences of decision and leadership, Martin Luther was the most gregarious of men and cannot be understood fully apart from an understanding of his friends and the part they played in his life. Whether one is dealing with his personal life or his theology, his leadership of the Reformation or his mixing in matters pertaining to the civil strife of princes and peasants, his marriage and family life or his translation of the Bible—in everything, his friends shared. In some cases they probably should have received more credit for the formulation of statements of position and actions taken than they have. In many cases, because of the strength of his leadership and personality, Luther is credited with the words and deeds of Melanchthon, Bugenhagen, Jonas, Amsdorf, and others.

This is, of course, a phenomenon whenever there is a strong and creative leader in any great movement. We should not, however, allow it to obscure the genuine contributions made by Luther's friends, as friends. The purpose here is not to provide evidence, nor even to suggest, that Luther was not the great leader that history has recognized. Whatever the contributions of his friends, they would be the first to insist on the priority of the one man as leader, as catalyst, as precipitant, and as champion.

Luther can best be understood in the circle of his friends. His blustery loudness must be seen against the background of tender concern for his own children and those of Melanchthon and Jonas. The real value of his Table Talk is that it was just that—genuine table talk, with his wife Katie hovering in back of his chair, and the normal give-and-take of conversation with one's peers. The

Wartburg "captivity" was effected at the hands of his friends, concerned about him personally, not just about his ideology. His first stirrings of revolt were within the friendly precincts of Staupitz's understanding and sympathy. His last words were to Justus Jonas, who had walked a long road with him.

There will be no disposition here to explain Luther's theology in terms of Melanchthon's formulation of it. Nor will I seek to explain the establishment of Lutheran organizational forms in Germany or Scandinavia as a result of the direction by "The Pomeranian," John Bugenhagen. I will not try to determine whether Luther could or could not have done his work without the comparatively loyal support of the Electors of Saxony. And who knows how decisive was the influence of Spalatin in securing the support of the Electors? It may be that a special study could be done on the relationship of Luther to Carlstadt and Zwilling and others who came to disagreement with the Reformer, and whether or not the break could have been avoided. These and like questions will not be answered, at least not as such. They will be touched upon and hinted at; they will be implied. But, basically we will be concerned with a demonstration of Luther as "socius," as a friend among friends.

Martin Luther made friends readily. In his own telling of it, he seemed to feel that his religious experience in the midst of a thunderstorm set him apart from other young men. However strange the incident may have seemed to Luther's friends, they attended the farewell party for him as he left the study of law to become a novice in the Augustinian monastery at Erfurt. Neither his rather serious turn of mind, nor his comparatively bizarre response to a frightening experience, kept him from normal friendly relationships.

Luther's basically friendly personality was evidenced even more clearly upon his entry into the life of a monk. One is tempted to declare that he did just about everything in his power to turn his fellows from him. The life was austere, but he carried austerity to the point of rebuke from his superiors. Periods of silence and meditation were incumbent upon all the monks; he turned them in upon himself with an intensity which made his prayers and devotional life a problem to all those who came into contact with him. Nevertheless, the thing that stands out above all else from this period is the response which others gave to him as a person.

Not only Staupitz, the monastery superior, but others of his companions demonstrated a concern for him, an interest born out of friendship. The friendship of Staupitz was so great a factor in the life of Luther that one can hardly understand the future Reformer's developing ideas and character except in the Vicar-General's sympathetic understanding and direction. From his association with the Augustinians, Luther built life-long friendships with Justus Jonas (then Jodocus Koch) of Nordlingen, Conrad Mutianus, Wenceslaus Link, Christopher Scheurl, and others.

Perhaps more should be said about a relationship which should have blossomed into friendship but did not. The greatest scholar of the time was Erasmus, of Rotterdam. His followers were in every University center, and his writings were among the decisive writings of our literate history. The "Enchiridion" and his Greek New Testament were the textbooks of a wave of humanistic learning that caught the imagination and intellect of whole generations. Through Philipp Melanchthon, Erasmus influenced the whole of the German Reformation. Yet he and Luther never met, and Erasmus carefully dissociated himself from the movement of reform after flirting with it briefly.

Luther began what relationship there was between the two with a characteristic approach. In 1516, George Spalatin, secretary to the Elector Frederick, wrote to Erasmus, telling him that a "young friend" thought he had misinterpreted St. Paul on justification by faith. That young friend was Martin Luther. The letter was set aside by Erasmus and never answered so far as we know. Whatever he may have thought about Luther's critical understanding, Erasmus wrote in 1518 to one of the Friar's friends, John Lang, not only with sympathetic interest in the Ninety-five Theses, but also indicating that he agreed with Luther in his feelings about abuses within the Church: "I see that the monarchy of the Pope in Rome, as it is now, is a pestilence to Christendom, but I do not know if it is expedient to touch that sore openly. That would be a matter for princes, but I fear that these will act in concert with the Pope to secure part of the spoils. . . . I do not know what possessed Eck to take up arms against Luther."

It is difficult to assess the record and to define the exact reasons why Erasmus and Luther moved in different directions. Melanchthon sought to bring the two together. Erasmus evidently appreciated Luther and his early work in biblical interpretation. On April 22, 1519, he wrote to Melanchthon from Louvain that "Luther's life is approved by everyone here: opinions differ concerning his learning. . . . Luther has rightly found fault with some things. Would that he had done so with a success equal to his courage." The same year, Melanchthon wrote to Erasmus: "Martin Luther is your convinced admirer and desires your full approbation." Yet, in this year of 1519, Erasmus made it plain to Melanchthon, Cardinal Campeggio, Jonas, and others that he did not belong to the movement of reform and that he remained faithful to the Catholic cause to the extent that he would not be led into any excesses. Luther was quite aware of the attitude of the great humanist, and while there was no open hostility, this was perhaps the starting point for the widening breach in a relationship that was never actually established.

Luther, however, still had much regard for Erasmus and his work in 1524. In that year, Melanchthon wrote to Erasmus with reference to a recent writing, "Diatribe," on his interpretation of the Bible. Interestingly enough, Melanchthon at one point in his letter says, "Luther is so angry as to get nothing out of it." But later he says, "I know his grateful feelings for you: it makes me hope he will answer you without delay. . . . Luther salutes you with respect." The respect didn't last. Nine years later, Luther was quite disenchanted with Erasmus's approach to the Reform Movement. In 1533, Erasmus wrote a book which he hoped would lead to peace in the Church, *De Sarcienda Ecclesia Concordia*. His plea for concessions had no appeal to Luther, however, who expressed himself with characteristic forcefulness: "Erasmus makes use of ambiguities intentionally and with malice."

Fundamentally, the two men were different in temperament and understanding. Perhaps it is too much to suggest that they might ever have come to terms. Luther was an activist who sensed, even where he did not see, the ultimate consequences of his words and actions and who nevertheless was willing to take what he believed to be the right steps. He seemed almost to glory in conflict, at least after the first open break with Rome. Erasmus, on the other hand, shrank from conflict of any kind. Concession and compromise were his weapons, and the longer a point of view was held, the greater its validity for him. He abhorred the physical violence and social and economic dislocation which came with the Reformation.

Whatever the reasons for the lack of sympathy between the two men, it was certainly a fact. One cannot help speculating about the course of history had Erasmus and Luther been friends. But Erasmus's desire to reserve himself "to be of use to the reviving studies" could not be reconciled with Luther's increasingly deeper split with the Church.

Erasmus's cautious withdrawal from the possibility of involvement came after receiving a letter from Luther inviting a closer relationship. Luther's letter, dated March 28, 1519, may have been, as some have suggested, a clever means of forcing the eminent humanist into a public avowal of a position which he intuitively expected him to take. In any case, this was the result. Erasmus wrote an answer a couple of months later, expressing indignation that people had accused him of being the author of some of Luther's works, and disclaiming even to have read any of the Wittenberg professor's writings. In this letter he definitely took a stand for "discreet moderation" as being more "likely to bring better progress than impetuosity." Discreet moderation was a long way from the leadership which Luther was giving right then, and even further from his activity in the years immediately ahead.

If Erasmus became disenchanted with the Reform Movement, this was not true of all the humanists, many of whom became followers and fast friends of Martin Luther. Nuremberg was one of the humanist centers whose leaders were important to the cause. There the Augustinians favored the humanist approach made familiar to them by Staupitz. The celebrated preacher and prior of the Augustinians was Wenceslaus Link, who was closely associated with the Lutherans for a number of years. Christopher Scheurl, a jurist who was close to Luther in later disputations, came from this group, beginning correspondence with the Reformer as early as 1516.

Among others were civic leaders such as Caspar Nutzel, who translated the Ninety-five Theses into German; Lazarus Spengler, a devoted follower of Luther; and Albrecht Dürer, the renowned painter, who demonstrated his affection for Luther by painting him as St. John, the beloved disciple. This should not be too surprising, since Luther was, in a very real sense, a product of humanist writing, particularly in his acquaintance with and use of Erasmus's New Testament. Whatever the developing relationship with Erasmus, others were being attracted to the banner and the person of Martin Luther. By 1518, he was making an impact in the Augustinian Order. When he went to Heidelberg for a chapter meeting, a customary public disputation was held, and Staupitz asked him to preside. His presentations were so reserved and scholarly in nature that even though many present did not agree with him, they were respectful and friendly in their treatment of him.

Especially impressed were several of the younger men, including Martin Bucer, who became one of the leading Reformers. It is Bucer who, writing to a friend, gives a glowing description of Luther at this time: "His charm in responding is amazing, his patience in listening is incomparable . . . he overcomes everyone with admiration." While Luther did not succeed in winning some of the older men who gradually turned from him because of their conviction that he was basically a troublemaker, he nevertheless was always with friends and making new ones. Because of the enmity aroused in some quarters through the publishing of the Theses, there was some fear for Luther's safety on the journey to and from Heidelberg. But his growing group of friends provided a circle of companions as he traveled. They wanted to be sure he got there and back.

Later in this same year, in October 1518, Luther was summoned to Augsburg to defend himself before the Papal Legate, Cardinal Cajetan. Again, his friends were concerned. They refused to let him go alone to the hearing, being suspicious of the Cardinal's intentions. Through Spalatin, a letter of safe-conduct was obtained from the Elector, but this did not fully allay fears for his safety. Luther himself thought he was doomed. Later he said, "I had the stake before my eyes constantly." The tremendous forces arrayed against him makes all the more significant his friends' determination to go with him. Wenceslaus Link, John Frosch, and three other monks were traveling companions, and John von Staupitz arrived to counsel with him.

The burden of Cajetan's appraisal of the situation was that Luther must recant. This Luther refused to do unless by Scripture he could be proved wrong in his understanding. The Cardinal became somewhat muddled in his argument, especially when challenged by Luther, and resorted to loud insistence that he recant. In a letter to Spalatin that day, Luther expressed his unalterable opposition to the demands of Cajetan. "I shall not recant one syllable." Then he added a characteristic note, "and I shall have my defense, which I presented today, printed so that he may be refuted throughout the whole Christian world if he continues to deal with me as outrageously as he has begun."

To others Luther expressed himself in more down-to-earth terms: "the Cardinal may be an able Thomist, but he is no clear Christian thinker, and so he is about as fit to deal with this as an ass is to play the harp."

Both Link and Staupitz spent time with the Cardinal, who made conciliatory offers to be carried to Luther. There was some indication that Link may have given the impression that Luther might change his point of view. This may have been out of concern for the safety of Brother Martin. Staupitz saw quite clearly the danger to Luther. In view of his own continued adherence to the Roman Church, his action shows his very real affection for the younger man for the shape of whose thinking he was to a substantial degree responsible. First he tried to raise money so that Luther could escape from Germany, with Paris in mind as a safe place. Unfortunately, none of his friends in Augsburg had money to spare. His next action was to release the monk from his vows of obedience, that is, to release him from any further responsibility to the Augustinian Order. Feeling convinced that the Cardinal would move against him as well as Luther, Staupitz gave Martin freedom to save himself, and then with Wenceslaus Link he quietly left the city.

Four days after Staupitz and Link had gone, Luther's friends in Augsburg decided that it was dangerous for him to remain there. Arrangements were made for the opening of a little gate in the city wall after dark. With the help of Canon Langermantal and others, Luther was able to leave, riding a horse provided by the friends.

As with the Augsburg experience, it is quite difficult for the modern Reader to sort out all the arguments and counter-arguments of the Leipzig Disputation. Coming in July 1519, the debate took place only after elaborate and intricate maneuvering by everyone concerned. Again, it is important to note that while Luther made his decision to participate even if a safe-conduct was not forthcoming, his friends had no intention of letting him enter the arena alone. The opening shots came in a proposal for debate between Eck, a quite capable disputant, and Carlstadt, one of the leading Wittenberg theologians. Luther saw clearly that the only reason for Eck's concern was his, Luther's, point of view, especially as made public in the Ninety-five Theses. Twelve of them in particular drew Eck's fire. In addition, there was the whole question of papal authority. With the consent of Duke George of Saxony and the faculty of Leipzig University, Luther prepared to defend his own propositions.

Carlstadt and Eck met in a preliminary session to determine the terms of the debate. Here Eck declared that he would insist upon the Italian style of debate, which called for free statement and reply. Luther's followers had expected not only to use the German style of disputation, but had anticipated the publication of written statements which would be used. The final agreement was to use the German style of debate, without publication of the results. Eck was not happy with that, since he was ready of tongue and wit but shallow in theological and biblical understanding. Luther was unhappy, too, since he rightly felt that the publication of arguments would find a good response among his countrymen.

The disputation began with Carlstadt and Eck the first week. For minds as unaccustomed as ours to theological disputation, it is somewhat strange to discover that during the hours of debate, some seventy-six burghers marched out each day with drums beating and the sounding of trumpets to keep the peace. The people of Leipzig were not favorable to the cause of Luther, a fact which was evidenced primarily in the favors shown to Eck, while ignoring the Wittenbergers. When Luther went to the lecturer's desk on July 4, Carlstadt had not done very well, perhaps because of an accident he suffered just as he arrived in Leipzig. Luther later wrote that Carlstadt "is laying up disgrace instead of honor."

That Carlstadt was not a successful disputant did not mean that Luther was now alone. Among his advisers was Melanchthon, who was fast becoming known as his best friend. Also representing his point of view was Nicholas Amsdorf (who was also with Luther at Worms), Eiserman, John Lang, Fachs, and a number of others. Duke Barnim, honorary rector of Wittenberg University, was one of those who traveled in two open wagons with Luther and Carlstadt to Leipzig. They were accompanied by about two hundred armed students, powerful evidence of the tremendous personal appeal of the Friar of Wittenberg. While he was doing his own talking, it was with the knowledge that there was a growing number of those who not only were captured by his reasoning, but captivated by him as well.

At the conclusion of the Disputation on July 14, Luther left Leipzig, with Eck feeling that he had done much the better by going with the Reformer. The people of Leipzig seemed to feel the same way, if we may judge by their generous response to Eck. Even in this period when he felt depressed, however, Luther discovered that Frederick the Elector, who had not yet strongly endorsed the movement of reform, was showing a friendliness which was to find expression many times in critical situations. When Eck sought the support of the Elector in his campaign against Luther, Frederick simply passed Eck's letter to Luther and Carlstadt themselves. At this same time, Luther was having a congenial meeting with Staupitz and Link, his superiors in the Augustinian Order. Staupitz remained to his last days a friend of Luther, while Link became a strong follower.

To read the record of the Reformation period is to sense a rapidly growing following for Luther which went beyond establishing the friendship of specific persons. A leading knight, Sickingen, offered in 1519 a place of refuge, and a hundred others offered protection. While Luther rejected such offers, feeling that he must carry out his mission and that his ultimate security was in God, come what might, he must have been heartened by such offers.

When Eck returned to Leipzig a year after the Disputation, he expected to have the same friendly reception accorded him on the earlier visit. Instead, the students and leaders of the University had turned cool, and lampoons were posted in a number of places about the town. The atmosphere had changed so much that he found it advisable to go into seclusion in a monastery, although even there he was not safe from threats and challenge. The change in attitude toward Eck was a reflection of the greater change of sympathies toward Luther. The coming of about fifty armed Wittenberg students for the

Michaelmas fair in Leipzig may have had something to do with the change.

While the events of 1518 and 1519 were transpiring, Luther was busy with his pen. Several of his writings stirred his opponents to make a series of strong pleas to Rome to have him branded as a heretic and his writings condemned. Two of the

Drawing of Luther as a young man by Cranach.

writings were especially influential: *A Prelude on the Babylonian Captivity of the Church* and *An Open Letter to the Christian Nobility of the German Nation Concerning the Reform of the Christian Estate*. In the latter document Luther enunciated the startling proposition—startling to a society which had for centuries accepted the doctrine of two estates, two powers, two laws—that there is only one estate, that of the believer. When a man has been baptized he is his own priest. No mediator is needed between the Christian and God. The priest is not needed for man to enter into relationship with God, and God certainly does not need the priest or any other human mediator to communicate with man. With this as his foundation, Luther went on to suggest that clergymen and princes alike are servants entrusted with responsibilities. Secular power cannot be used to compel in spiritual matters, only in temporal affairs. Clergymen are entrusted their powers by their fellows, and these powers also may be withdrawn by them.

Obviously, such teaching was anathema to the Church. Its whole structure was threatened. In Germany in particular, with the ferment of nationalism, the princes felt a strong undergirding for their proposals for self-determination, both as regarded by the Church and by the empire. The Pope had established a commission a year before to deal with Luther. Although Cajetan, one member of the commission, had been able to slow down the process somewhat, by June 1520 a bull of condemnation, *Exsurge Domine*, was published, giving Luther sixty days to recant or submit to authority.

During all the negotiations in the Curia at Rome, Luther's friends had supported him by every means. Some became more open in their acceptance of his teachings. Mention has been made of the growing response from students and University faculties. This should not lead to the assumption that there was no opposition of any kind. But there is no question that public support, and, more important in many respects, the support of the princes was increasingly manifested. When the Pope tried to get at Luther through the Elector Frederick, the Elector simply passed the Pope's letters on to Luther, at the same time using every stratagem for gaining time and blunting the Pope's efforts. As more and more of the princes sided with Luther, his support became formidable indeed.

One of the decisive acts of defiance on the part of Luther was his burning of the Papal Bull and books of canon law at the Easter gate in Wittenberg, December 10, 1520. His act had the support of his many friends, so that what could easily have led to martyrdom instead indicated the tremendous following of the Friar. His friends were there, cheering the burning. At the same time, the Elector and others in authority refused to support the aggressive actions of Aleander, the Pope's representative, who had promoted an earlier burning of Luther's writings.

The whole incident is interesting from several aspects. Aleander had made a determined effort to secure the burning of the Reformer's books at several centers of learning and ecclesiastical authority, including Louvain, Liege, and Cologne. In the first two cities he was successful, but when he entered Germany proper, he discovered that the temper of the people and rulers was quite different. The Elector Frederick flatly refused to hear his proposals, listening instead to Erasmus, who happened to be in Cologne at the time. Erasmus had not yet come to a real parting of the ways with Luther, and he gave full support to the Elector in his rejection of Aleander. His summary of the situation gave the Elector some merriment: "Luther has committed two sins. He has attacked the crown of the Pope, and the bellies of the monks." The decision of the Elector was that Luther's works should not be burned until he had been convicted of error. On November 12, after the Elector's departure from Cologne, Aleander went ahead with the burning of what he thought were Luther's books. However, as at Louvain, where the students had gathered a number of meaningless books and some old sermons, Luther's supporters in Cologne had arranged that only bundles of waste paper were burned. In Mainz the result was quite the same. The students there took charge of the fire and saw to it that anti-Luther writings were burned instead of Luther's books.

All of this was conveyed to Luther by his friends. When Spalatin visited him at Wittenberg, Luther announced in the pulpit his intention of burning the papal decrees and that he was ready to burn the Bull publicly. Spalatin, devoted secretary to the Elector, reported to Frederick and asked if he had any objections. It is a measure of the friendliness of "the old fox" that he refrained from any negative action.

The burning of the Papal Bull and canon law books most likely took place on December 10, because that was the date ending the period of grace allowed Luther for recanting. Melanchthon posted a notice of the coming bonfire, inviting the public to the burning of the "impious works of papal law and scholastic theology . . . according to ancient and apostolic usage." Agricola scoured the town for as many of the "impious works" as he could find. Probably it was Agricola who built up the kindling and fired it. After several volumes of canon law had been thrown on the fire, Luther stepped up and threw upon the flames a small booklet in which the Papal Bull may have been inserted. There could be reason to doubt whether the Bull was actually burned, except that Luther wrote specifically about it to Spalatin, and Agricola gives a personal report. Other witnesses were students and faculty of the University.

The most significant part of the whole proceeding was the burning of the books of canon law, which was for the people of the time comparable to the commandments of God. From now on, Rome could have no doubt as to the seriousness of the situation. Many who had been at least somewhat friendly to Luther turned against him, recognizing his act for what it was, a definite break with Roman authority and a defiance of its basic point of view. The day before the burning, Knight Hutten proposed an alliance with Luther in open revolt against the Church. The alliance was rejected by Luther, but the burning of canon law was a clear indication that the revolt had begun. Not only Hutten, but the people of Germany, understood the terms of the conflict. In February 1521, Aleander reported to the Curia that all of Germany was in revolt, with nine-tenths in support of Luther and the remaining one-tenth opposed to Rome, even if indifferent to Luther.

So it was that the friends of Luther found their ranks constantly increasing. Erasmus, along with many of the purely humanist scholars, from this time on found reasons to withdraw from association with the Reform Movement. But they were replaced by individuals unknown except by their numbers, as well as many who were prominent in university, church, and civil life. Electors, princes, knights, professors, students, clergymen, and ordinary persons were counted among the followers of Luther. From time to time Luther spoke and wrote as though he was in danger of martyrdom, but the numbers and status of his friends increasingly ruled out this possibility.

Perhaps best known of all the experiences of Luther in which his friends played a part was the Diet on Worms and its aftermath. The details are fairly well known. Charles V, fearful for his ambitious imperial plans if he could not have control of the German princes, opened the Diet on January 27, 1521. In attendance were representatives of the free cities and leading nobles and clergy. Immediately the question of Martin Luther assumed central importance. Forces had been gathering on both sides. The Cardinals of Mainz, Salzburg, and Sitten, plus their followers—representing the support of Pope Leo X and the Curia—wanted Charles to condemn Luther. The Pope's support of Charles came only after he found that the German princes, led by the Elector Frederick the Wise, were in favor of Charles in his contest with Francis I of France for the throne as Holy Roman Emperor.

On the other side were Luther and the German princes, along with Luther's loyal friends in the universities and the monasteries. The princes were not, at least at the outset, supporters of Luther, but they were opposed to any effort by Charles to override the growing national self-consciousness of the German people and states. They would not surrender the Reformer if it meant the abrogation of the powers which they considered to be reserved to themselves. And it did not take them long to discover that in the teaching and doctrines of the Reformer was the rationale which was ultimately their own greatest strength.

The trip to Worms was financed by a gift from the University at Wittenberg, and the town council placed at Luther's disposal the wagon of one Christian Döring, along with three horses to pull it. When the money from the University ran out, the supply was replenished by Duke John, brother of the Elector. Riding with Luther in the wagon were Nicholas Amsdorf, a student from Pomerania named Peter Suave, and a traveling brother of the Augustinians, John Petzensteiner. At every town the little party was announced by the imperial herald, and swarms of people came out to see this Friar who "had been so daring as to set himself against the Pope and the whole world." Many agreed that he was on his way to his own funeral pyre. Their conviction did not dissuade him from continuing on his journey, however.

Various towns invited him to preach in their churches, and Luther took these opportunities to restate his opinions concerning the Pope and the Church and of priests in general. There is considerable evidence that the Emperor and his advisors hoped to delay Luther long enough so that the imperial safe-conduct would expire and leave Martin vulnerable to apprehension. However, Luther sensed what they had in mind and resolutely traveled on, arriving in Worms on the morning of the last day of the safe-conduct, April 16, 1521.

The town of Worms had a population of some seven thousand at the time, and contemporary accounts suggest that several hundred went out to greet the Reformer. Among these were a number of prominent noblemen and clerics who had come to Worms to stand publicly with Luther. When the little entourage came through the appropriately named Martin's Gate into the city, Justus Jonas became part of Luther's company. Theirs was a close friendship that was to continue to the end of Luther's life, with Jonas as his companion in his last moments.

The only friends available to Luther during the two days of his appearance before the Diet were Amsdorf and Spalatin, the Elector's secretary. Amsdorf had to stay under cover, since he did not have a safe-conduct and was continually in danger. Spalatin, because of his connection with the Elector, who was not publicly supporting Luther, was forced to be very circumspect in his every action. Probably his chief help was to instruct Luther in the proper conduct and presentation to the Emperor and the princes. Luther had the option of consulting with Amsdorf and Spalatin and knew they supported him at every point. After Luther's famous appearance, with his "Here I stand . . . God help me! Amen," Jerome Schurf joined Amsdorf in support of Luther in his discussions with John Cochleus and others who sought to persuade Luther to recant. The efforts, as every Reader of history knows, were unavailing, and Luther was given a safe-conduct of twenty-one days for his return to Wittenberg. Again, friendship had been demonstrated when the pressures were great; relationships were cemented which continued throughout the Reformer's life.

Knowing that the safe-conduct was likely to be violated, Luther's friends took matters into their own hands. While the Elector Frederick had not wished to go too far in support of Luther lest he mistake the will of God, he was not, on the other hand, willing "to have himself burdened with the emperor either." So, he made arrangements to have Luther spirited away during his return journey. The Elector refrained from asking his counselors where they were going to take Luther, so that he could honestly say, when asked, that he did not know what had happened to him. Bernard von Hirschfeld and several others who had ridden out to meet the Friar's party as they approached Worms on April 16 were the leaders of a small group of horsemen who began to escort him on the trip back home. The whole affair was evidently rehearsed, though not even Amsdorf, among Luther's traveling companions, knew what was going to happen.

Petzensteiner was badly frightened when five armed horsemen set upon the party, and disappeared into the woods. Amsdorf set up a loud clamor, which effectively covered the "kidnapping," and Luther was hurriedly "forced" to accompany his captors to the Wartburg. There he was given a knight's clothing; he let his tonsure grow, along with his beard, and became the knight: Junker George. The whole affair at Worms, with the Wartburg aftermath, Luther's life and movements—all were in the hands of his friends. They supported him publicly when their own lives could have been forfeit. They boldly planned for keeping him and his leadership alive. During his residence in the Wartburg he busied himself with his translation of the New Testament from its original Greek, and he kept himself informed of the progress of the Reform Movement through his friends.

Actually, during this period Luther's friends took on new significance for the Reformation. At Wittenberg, it was Melanchthon, Carlstadt, and Zwilling who gave form and substance to the movement. In the last few months of 1521 and the first part of 1522, monks, priests, and nuns married, sometimes each other. The liturgy was reformed, with Melanchthon administering both bread and wine at communion to students in September 1521. Amidst much violence producing action, Justus Jonas proposed the abolition of vigils and private Masses. Subsequently, statues were removed from the churches, and other reform actions were taken.

Luther was in agreement with much of what was happening, but he was greatly opposed to the violence which flared up from time to time. He was particularly irritated by the leadership of Carlstadt and Zwilling in much of the violence. Because of this, he was soon alienated from both of them. During his "exile," Luther depended chiefly on Melanchthon and Spalatin. Melanchthon kept him informed concerning the movement itself, and Spalatin kept him informed of its effect upon the Elector Frederick. It must have been a most difficult thing for the Elector to continue his support of the reforms when the friends of Luther embarrassed him so greatly by their excesses.

From this point on, there is evidence of more than friendship for Luther among his supporters; they became his colleagues and collaborators in the ever-widening Reform Movement. Some of them were so influential in their own right that they became spokesmen for whole segments of the movement, and upon occasion, for Luther himself.

In 1529, Philip of Hesse believed the time had come to have agreement among the main Reformers. To this end he invited the Swiss Reformers Zwingli and Oecolampadius, the Strassburger, Bucer, and the German leaders, Luther and Melanchthon, to meet at his castle overlooking Marburg to work out a common confession. He was hopeful that this would lead to a political confederation and would settle an acrimonius debate about Holy Communion.

While Luther was suspicious of the idea of a political confederation, he was willing to talk about a common confession of faith. For several days in October 1529, they debated at Marburg, although from the beginning there was little hope of ultimate agreement. Luther began by writing on a table with chalk the words "this is my body," indicating the only understanding with which he would agree concerning the Lord's Supper. Actually, there was agreement on fourteen of fifteen points of discussion, and Luther was ready to agree to inter-communion with the other branches of the Reform Movement. Here, though, Melanchthon became most influential among the Germans, urging Luther to steer clear of the idea of intercommunion. His reasoning was based upon his feeling that there was still hope for reconciliation with Catholicism. Therefore his desire was to avoid moving too far from the Catholic view of the Sacrament.

Today there is a painting in the room where this "Marburg Colloquy" took place, with a lively depiction of the interest with which the disputants took part in the discussion. One would have thought this was a golden opportunity for the various reform elements to reach consensus. Such was not the case, although later events justify the view that Luther could well have resisted the suggestions of Melanchthon at this point. It is of interest to note that all those present, including Luther, put their signatures to the fourteen of fifteen points on which there was agreement.

But this did not by any means indicate that Luther was in a friendly frame of mind toward those who opposed him in the matter of interpreting the Lord's Supper. Jonas, Cruciger, Myconius, Brenz, Osiander, and Agricola were present as his friends and colleagues. But Zwingli and all those who agreed with his interpretation were condemned to utmost darkness. Luther rejected the proffered hand of Zwingli saying, "Your spirit is not our spirit." Several days later Luther wrote concerning the Swiss Reformers, "They are not only liars, but the very incarnation of lying, deceit, and hypocrisy." So the Marburg Colloquy, while drawing the lines of leadership for the German Reformation, effectively shut out the possibility of a joint enterprise with the Swiss.

The impressive influence of Melanchthon was evident less than a year later when the Emperor, Charles V, called for a Diet at Augsburg, which Luther could not attend, being under imperial ban. At Augsburg, the German princes made a firm stand for the Reformation principles, a stand taken in the face of possible loss of position, prestige, and properties, and therefore most notable. After the nobles had made their position clear, a statement of reform principles, drawn up by Melanchthon, was presented to express their views.

This statement, known from then on as the "Augsburg Confession," was Melanchthon's effort to minimize the differences between Catholic and Protestant, and to demonstrate how far the German Reformers were from the Swiss. Luther, safely ensconced at Coburg on the Saxony border, another of the Elector's castles, was not happy at first with Melanchthon's work, believing that he had made too many concessions. Later, Melanchthon made changes in a second draft of the Confession, and it continues to the present as a basic statement of belief for Lutherans worldwide. In the course of the discussions concerning the Confession, after it was signed by the theologians representing the Reformers as well as the Protestant princes, Melanchthon had occasion to give an impressive display of personal conviction and courage. In a heated exchange with Campeggio, the Papal Legate, the Protestants were roundly condemned. Melanchthon's answer deserves to be placed alongside Luther's stand at Worms: "We cannot yield, nor can we desert the truth, and we pray for the sake of God and Christ that our adversaries will concede to us that which we cannot with a good conscience relinquish. . . . To God we will commit our cause and ourselves! If God be for us, who can stand against us?"

During the almost six months of theological wrangling in the preparation of the Augsburg Confession and the period of discussion after the presentation, Luther was at Coburg studying, praying, and writing to Melanchthon and others who were in the thick of it. While his influence was constantly felt, the basic decisions were those of Melanchthon and the other Protestant theologians who worked with him. Master Philipp not only demonstrated his Erasmian leaning, but sturdy convictions of his own as well. While the Swiss Reformers were excluded from consideration during the course of the presentation of the Confession, they presented confessions of their own, as did the representatives of Strasbourg and other communities.

The Augsburg Confession was not signed by those who were outside the mainstream of the German Reformation, but it became a bulwark of Protestantism nevertheless in the long struggle with Rome. It is further testimony of the importance of the friends of Martin Luther for his life and work.

During this period, Luther's Reformation was taking hold throughout many sections of Germany, with the princes and other civil rulers taking the lead in some cases, in others, following the lead of the people. A number of Luther's friends and coworkers were prominent in the spread of his teachings: Bugenhagen became the Reformer for Pomerania, as well as being a leader in the spread of Luther's teaching doctrines in Scandinavia; Capito, and then Bucer, carried the Reform Movement to Strassburg and Ulm. Basically it was men who had studied under Luther at the University in Wittenberg, or who were associated with him in the Augustinian Order, who were the leaders in the ever-expanding Reformation. Many of these friends of the Friar of Wittenberg found it hard to remain constant, due to his increasingly temperamental outbursts as he grew older. Nevertheless, most maintained their loyalty even though they sometimes avoided his presence. At times even the relationship with the gentle Melanchthon was strained, although to the time of the death of Luther there was no open break. Luther was not easy to work with.

On occasion, Luther went along with the judgment of a friend, even though his own better judgment warned him against it. In 1539, Landgrave Philip, of Hesse, decided to take Margaret von de Saale as a wife, even though he was already married to Christina of Saxony by whom he had six children. Philip continually had trouble restraining his passion and thought that a second wife, for whom he had real affection, might curb it. Obviously, such a bigamous proposition could not but offend Catholics and Protestants alike. The Landgrave consulted with Bucer, who proposed support for Philip's action from Luther, Melanchthon, and other leading Reformers.

While there were political overtones to the affair, since Philip evidently gave some impression that he might defect to the Catholics, Melanchthon, who wrote the opinion on which action was formally based, seems to have been primarily concerned with biblical rationalization. He proposed the idea of the lesser of two evils: it would be less evil for Philip to resort to bigamy than to continue in persistent immorality. It should be remembered that this type of thinking was not new; it had been proposed in the consistory as a solution for Henry VIII's marital difficulty earlier. Melanchthon reasoned that bigamy was not condemned in the Old Testament, that it was practiced in the New Testament, and that upon occasion the Church had given consent to it in the past.

Actually, Melanchthon and Luther seemed to be saying that bigamy is wrong, but if the necessity is great enough, the bigamist will not be held morally accountable for it. They evidently were aware of the implications of their action, yet they went ahead. In any case, the Landgrave took the opinion of Melanchthon as support for his desired action, and the marriage took place. The document which Melanchthon prepared was signed by him as well as Luther, Bucer, and six other well-known theologians. Because of the part played by the Reformers, ridicule came to the movement, not only from Catholics but from Protestants as well. It was not a happy time for the Reformation. The most one can say is that even when they did things wrong, Luther and his friends stayed together.

Even though Luther became more and more cantankerous in his later years, his dear friends remained loyal. The Reformer in his last few years had many bouts of sickness, forcing him to be dependent upon his friends to carry more and more responsibility in the movement. His illnesses were such that he seldom traveled alone. In 1546 he was in Eisleben, his birthplace, settling a dispute between the Counts of Mansfeld. The weather had been cold and he became quite ill. At two o'clock in the morning, on February 18, he called his friends to his room where he had lain down on a couch. Coelius, pastor at Mansfeld, one of the Countesses of Mansfeld, two of Luther's sons, and Justus Jonas were present. Jonas leaned over him and asked if he would "stand by Christ and the doctrine" he had preached. Luther's "yes" in response was one of his last words. On February 22, Bugenhagen preached the funeral sermon in the City Church at Wittenberg. Melanchthon gave a Latin oration.

There has been no intention here to evaluate the status of any particular friend in the life of Martin Luther. There is not much question that, with all their differences, Melanchthon was a great friend and confidante, beloved and trusted. He was, however, but one of a number of strong and capable men who made valuable contributions to the Reformation. Luther was for them a leader, and they were proud to call themselves his followers. The relationship was, however, more than that of leader and followers: these were his friends and companions. To them he was not Doctor Luther, but Brother Martinus. Consideration of Luther's relationship to his friends is a way to better understand him.

CHAPTER 3

John von Staupitz

It is not only important but necessary to excurse briefly into the life of Luther in order to get to know his friends and the meaning of their friendship with him. Although many of their lives have been covered in biographies, they really can be best appreciated and understood in their relationship with the Reformer. It is this relationship that gives them a place in history.

While other friends of Luther became Reformers, Staupitz was not one of them. He dedicated his life early to the Roman Catholic Church and never forsook it, though he sometimes veered as far away from the Church as possible, without taking the fatal last step toward the abyss into which the Church consigned all those who dared question its policies and practices. Luther told Melanchthon that he himself might die as a result of his teaching, but Staupitz took the same chance and no one seems to have thought much about it at the time. Much of Luther's theology that was contrary to the Church's teachings in its inception can be traced to the influence of Staupitz.

This does not mean, however, that Staupitz anticipated the outcome of Luther's thought, or that Luther did not himself make great contributions to the theology of the Reformation. It means that he built directly on the foundation which was his from Staupitz. The fact that Staupitz, with possibly one exception, never differed from Luther in his essential doctrines, seems to be at least prima facie evidence that, had he cared to risk his neck by doing so, he would have carried his interpretations as far as Luther did.

The name of Staupitz is so unfamiliar that we need to place him in historical perspective. When Luther was two years old, John von Staupitz matriculated at Leipzig University. In 1497 he was a Reader in Theology and Master of Arts at Tübingen. In 1503 he became Vicar of the German Province of the Augustinian Order of Eremites. In this same year, he was called to be Dean of the Faculty of Theology at the new University at Wittenberg. It was here that he received his Doctor of Divinity degree in 1510. His relationship with Martin Luther was very close, and it was he who twice influenced Luther to come to Wittenberg to study and later to teach.

Although Staupitz was unable or unwilling to follow Luther in his revolt from Rome, he was so much in sympathy with him that he left his position as Vicar August 28, 1520, and retired to Salzburg. By special dispensation from the Pope, he was allowed to leave the Augustinians for the Benedictines, becoming Abbot of the monastery of this Order in Salzburg until his death, shortly after Christmas 1524.

When Luther came to Wittenberg to teach in the Faculty of Theology, he was already a friend of Staupitz. He was one of the Augustinian monks who came under the direct personal supervision of Staupitz in his capacity as Vicar-General of the

German Province. Historians generally agree that Staupitz gave much attention to the young monk. This was entirely within the character of the man, as we get the picture at this late date and through rather meager sources. Perhaps there were some monks and monasteries that were given to licentiousness and loose living, but this was not true of those under the care and supervision of John von Staupitz.

In the middle of the Thirteenth Century there had been a split between the members of the Augustinian brotherhood in Germany regarding following lines of laxity and strictness in observance of the rules of the Order. The immediate predecessor of Staupitz as Vicar-General of the Observantine Union of the Order was Andreas Proles. He had been the leader in the fight for strict observance of the rules in the time just before Luther and his contemporaries, the fight which gave the name to this group: Observantine. The reformed branch was opposed to the Conventuals, or those who favored more laxity in the rule. Staupitz was no mean Reformer himself, for the very next year after becoming Vicar-General, he revised the constitution in favor of even greater stringency of discipline. This provided for the tonsure, examinations, minutia of discipline and conduct under the preceptor to which Luther, as a novice and as a professed monk, became subject.

The conflict between strict and more relaxed observance of monastic regulations among the Augustinians in Germany was evident in other Orders and centers as well. Girolamo Savonarola, one of the "Reformers before the Reformation," reorganized the Congregation of the Dominicans in Tuscany with the same aim as that of Proles and Staupitz in creating the Augustinian Eremites in Germany. Not only Luther's theology, but his profound discontent and disgust with the whole body of the clergy and Church practice received impetus through contact with the Vicar-General.

No period in the life of Luther has received more attention by critics than when he was a monk under Staupitz's influence. It is from Staupitz that we get a picture of Luther at this time: "He was not concerned with women but with real spiritual difficulties." Staupitz was Luther's confessor, and thus no one was in better position than he to know the innermost workings of the young novice's mind. The struggling soul of Luther was seeking for certainty. He tried all manner of penance and fasting, wasting away his body in a vain effort to find peace.

Luther imagined more sins and evils than would seem possible to most. He was called a "young saint" by the nuns from a nearby convent, but was probably at the very moment whispering to himself, as he often did, that he was "gallows-ripe." Once, when he was tormenting himself over sins that were no sins, an old professor brought him up sharply with the admonition: "You are a fool. God is not angry with you; it is you who are angry with God." In spite of temporary alleviations of his spiritual depression by various brothers, he had no permanent relief until he was taken in hand by the Vicar-General.

Staupitz was no far-off, distant overseer of spiritual life. He took an active interest in the monk with the emaciated face and the look of settled despair, and thereby came to know and admire Luther. He himself once remarked that he had never felt such troubles but that they were more necessary to Brother Martin than food and drink.

The interest of the Vicar-General in Luther, although a special one, did not mean that it was unique for Staupitz. He took an active lead in the life and affairs of all the monks under his charge, to the end that the local Augustinian congregation became known for strictness in fulfilling its vows and obligations. One has only to remember the conditions which were typical of the Church at large in that day to see that Staupitz must indeed have been a dedicated and devout leader of those in his care. Luther gratefully acknowledged at a later time the spiritual profit which he derived from Staupitz.

Although the Vicar-General was a leader in the group that insisted upon strict observance of the rules and vows, he believed the spirit was greater than the letter of the law. One imagines him sensitive to the troubled countenance of his colleague Luther, inquiring about the cause of his depression. These conversations at the study table must have been good for Luther and perhaps were a precursor of his own Table Talk. Staupitz was a cultured, urbane nobleman, welcome in sophisticated circles, yet he took time to inquire into problems of his most enigmatic novice while at the humble board of an Augustinian monastery. He was not afraid to relax when the occasion was a proper one. He is said to have kept as his motto, "Reverent at worship; merry at table." Although the cloister rules required silence at meals, it is likely that the spirit of the motto prevailed. Luther himself tells us that Staupitz could tell a pleasant story at mealtime, as well as edify his listeners with his more serious table talk.

There can be no doubt that Staupitz was understanding and sympathetic in the seclusion of the confessional, even as he was full of common sense in his other relationships with the monks. The very fact that Luther lays such stress on the help he received in the confessional argues in favor of this. Nowadays, Staupitz would get credit as a psychologist because of his treatment of Luther. With great skill he determined the source of the problems confronting Luther; then he prescribed remedies. In helping Luther solve his problems, he drew upon his own experiences. He was humane and understanding not only of the perplexities that arise in the minds of others, but of the things in his own life which helped him survive when the need arose.

Luther "unburdened his soul" over and over to Staupitz, telling him that the doctrine of predestination worried him and he feared eternal damnation. Luther's inability to achieve in his own life assurance that he had done sufficient to win the mercy of Christ bothered Staupitz. He was always gentle and to the point in his efforts to help Luther see the introspective quality of his meditations and to direct him to historical and actual realities.

Staupitz reviewed his own life and his own struggle with predestination. He reminded Luther of the wounds of Christ and told him to view the divine decree in the light of the salvation that was his through Christ. The Vicar-General had received this insight through the works of Gerson and Bernard, who found in the Cross their great reassurance in the face of doubt and trial—the guarantee of God's mercy and goodness. This Staupitz passed on to Luther. He frankly acknowledged the futility of seeking to attain to the perfect love of God by legalisms; he told his penitent that he had ceased to keep up this pretense and thus to try to please God. He told Luther of his daily confessions and daily resolutions to always serve God perfectly. And he told him of his daily failures until he determined to give up what must be a lie in the sight of God and to wait for God's grace. Without God's grace, all is lost.

Penitential practice, according to Staupitz, was based on a mistaken principle. Penitence ought to spring from the love of God and his righteousness, not regarded as the means of attaining God's love. This, Staupitz believed, was an impossible undertaking and could only foster a sense of failure, with resultant self-torment and misery. The love of God is the beginning rather than the goal of true penitence. All of this came out of Staupitz's own experience. For this reason Staupitz's counsel was peculiarly fitted to the similar experience of the young

Luther. In 1542, Luther wrote to Count Albert of Mansfeld of his difficulties over the problems of predestination, which gave rise to speculation and religious questioning: "I also was so entangled in these speculations and trials that if Dr. Staupitz, or rather God through Dr. Staupitz, had not helped me out of them, I would have been overwhelmed and long since in Hell."

When Luther wrote to him, "O my sin, my sin, my sin!" Staupitz replied, "You wish to be without sin, and you have no real sin. Christ is the forgiveness of genuine sins like parricide, sacrilege, adultery, and so on. Those are true sins. You must have a catalogue of real sins, if Christ is to help you. You must not go about with such trifles and trumpery and make a sin out of every inadvertence."

Staupitz was not only wise and gentle with Luther, he was firm and told him he did not know what was the matter with him. But constant study of the problem of the young Augustinian gradually made him aware of the real problem which Luther would have to overcome, and he suggested to him the solution. He delivered him from the fear that he was a reprobate by convincing him that his sins were sent to him for his own good, in order to train him for an important career—another suggestion that probably resulted from his own earlier struggles. It was through his Vicar-General that Luther came to believe so completely in a God who was merciful, who forgave freely those who threw themselves upon Christ in faith and ceased to trust in their own merits. This is the one truth that has buoyed up men of faith for centuries. This is the truth that found a guarantor in Staupitz's life but to which Luther had been blind until his eyes were opened by his confessor and spiritual advisor.

Perhaps the greatest thing that Staupitz did for Luther was to point out to him that he was right in setting over against each other the righteousness of God and the sin and helplessness of man, but that he was wrong when he kept these in permanent opposition. God had promised that man could have fellowship with him. All fellowship is founded on personal trust. And trust—that is, trust of the believer—in a personal God who has promised grace and forgiveness, brings one into that fellowship with God through which all things that belong to God can become his.

Without this personal trust, which we call faith, all divine things—the Incarnation and Passion of the Savior, the Word and the Sacraments—however true as matters of fact, are outside man and cannot be truly possessed. But when man trusts God and his promises, and when the fellowship which trust or faith brings about is once established, then these divine things may be truly possessed by the man who trusts. The just live by their faith.

These concepts indicate the extent to which the theology of Staupitz was the forerunner of Luther's theology. The assurance that Luther gained from Staupitz dispelled much of the gloom from his soul, even as the hard-won beliefs had once dispelled the gloom from the soul of Staupitz himself.

Wise counselor that he was, Staupitz was also an educator and administrator. His administrative ability was shown earlier in his relations with the Augustinian Order. Facing the split between the two branches of the Order in Germany in 1509, Staupitz, in his official capacity in the Eremite or Observantine Union, suggested a plan for bringing the two branches into harmony, thus strengthening their efforts in the assault upon the world. The opposition did not come from the Conventuals where it was expected. One might expect that they would have wanted to retain their laxity, but this does not seem to have been the case.

The opposition came from the Observantines, evidently out of fear that they could not maintain the strictness which they felt was necessary for the proper disciplining of the spirit. The plan, favored by Staupitz, included a union of the opposing factions in the provinces of Saxony and Thuringia only. It was sanctioned by a Papal Bull, issued in 1510, although the Bull had actually been drawn up in 1507. This Bull of Union had no effect on the brothers, who kept right on in their division. Because Staupitz pressed the matter, John Nathin, Luther's old preceptor at Erfurt, and Luther were sent to the Archbishop of Magdeburg to present the objections of the brothers to the union.

When the efforts at Halle met with no success, the delegation of two was sent to Rome to present their objections to the General of the Order. It must have been a source of satisfaction to Staupitz to have his protégé as one of the members of this mission, though Luther was one of the most fervid opponents of the case for the union, since he was a strict disciplinarian himself. And, in spite of the efforts at Rome by Luther and his colleague, Staupitz does not seem to have borne them any ill-will. The plan for union did not succeed because of the opposition offered by the Erfurt brothers, and Staupitz himself decided that there was no further use in pressing the matter, dropping the agitation in 1512.

In spite of what could have been cause for a rift between the two, Luther came to the monastery at Wittenberg at the express desire of Staupitz, and Staupitz was big enough to see to it that Luther became sub-prior of the monastery, recognizing the abilities possessed by the young monk. He again showed his generosity of spirit and his insight into the character of Luther when he selected him to be his successor as teacher of Bible at the University of Wittenberg. Luther's move from Erfurt in 1508 was also due to the continual bickering among the monks, while at Wittenberg there was an air of good fellowship and conciliation that was more conducive to creative activity.

All the while he was receiving the marks of signal favor from Staupitz, it must be remembered that Luther was apparently opposed to the plan of union within the Augustinian Order, prized by Staupitz. The greatness of the student has overshadowed the magnanimous spirit of the teacher, which helped make possible the fruition of that greatness.

The quality of the abilities of Staupitz is shown again by his work with the infant University of Wittenberg. Frederick the Elector had maintained close relations with the Augustinian Eremites ever since he had made their acquaintance while a schoolboy at Grimma, and the Vicar-General, Staupitz, along with Dr. Pollich of Mellerstadt, were his chief advisers. Hence it was no surprise that Staupitz was called to a post of importance when the Elector decided to found a new University at Wittenberg to offset the influence of the University at Leipzig. The University was established so that the Elector could have everything in his province that his brother had in his.

Staupitz was made Dean of the Faculty of Theology. Although the school was opened under Imperial Privilege of Maximilian, the Holy Roman Emperor, it seems to have seen some dark days before Luther and his coterie made it a power in German education. The town was small and poor, and the students were loathe to trust their future careers to a school of no reputation. Staupitz went on recruiting trips to the various Augustinian monasteries and collected promising young monks who were enrolled as students. The school opened in 1502 with some 416 students enrolled, a somewhat artificial success. By 1505, the summer session, the roll had shrunk to 56. When Frederick would have closed the doors of the institution, Staupitz urged him to persevere. Luther was sent to teach Dialectic and the Physics of Aristotle but was urged after he arrived to study Bible in order that he might teach in that field.

The requirements of the doctorate for which Luther studied included preaching. Luther told the Dean that studying and preaching simultaneously were too much for him and that in three months he would be dead. To this the Dean replied, speaking from experience, that he, too, had shrunk from holding forth in the pulpit. He made fun of Luther's plea that he would soon be dead from the duties incumbent on a preacher, doctor, and teacher: "In God's name, then, let it be so. Our Lord God has very important business at hand in heaven and has great need of you up there." So he laughed him into the pulpit of the monastery.

All the while he was teaching, Staupitz had the affairs of the Order to think of, in addition to guiding the perplexed students and tending to the many details of University administration. When Luther graduated into the doctorate, and was unable to pay the required fee, Staupitz went to his friend, the Elector, and asked him to pay the fifty gulden, which he did. Even as late as 1519, Luther had to fall back on the support of his teacher. To Martin Glaser, from whom he had borrowed a horse (and forgotten to return it), he wrote, "I hope you will be indulgent to a poor man like me in the affair of your horse, on account of the intercession of the Venerable Father Staupitz. . . . I hope we may see you here again, as I am glad to learn from Staupitz is likely to be the case." One is tempted to generalize that the great become so because of their tendency to neglect smaller details and amenities, while the near-great remain just that because they are too busy with details to achieve greatness.

While Erasmus was able to remain neutral in the controversies which marked the early years of the Reformation, his followers and those most famous for their devotion to his principles were not so fortunate. Staupitz was a frequent supporter of the humanism of the Dutch scholar, as were Emser, Murner,

Spalatin, and others. Emser and Murner were among those who turned against Luther, while Spalatin remained one of the Reformer's most influential friends as secretary and chaplain to the Elector Frederick.

Staupitz, in his teaching of theology, was moved by his humanist training to sometimes differ from the traditional theology of the Church, as he did on the question of penance. He urged Luther to become, as he himself was, a good localis and textualis in the Bible; that is, one who, when he met with difficulties in the interpretation, did not content himself with commentaries but made collections of parallel passages for himself, and found explanations of the one in the others. In thus teaching Luther to think for himself in the best humanist tradition, Staupitz was giving him the weapon with which he was to break through the dogmatisms of the Church.

Among other reasons why Luther was called to Wittenberg to teach was that Staupitz knew of his humanist tendencies. The interest of the Dean in humanism is suggested again by the fact that it was considered quite a feather in his cap when young Philipp Melanchthon was called, at the age of twenty-two, to lecture in Greek at the small University. That Staupitz tempered his humanism with evangelicalism is indicated by the fact that no group gave Luther more enthusiastic support than the Nuremberg humanists. Led by a few ardent admirers of Staupitz, one of whom was Wenceslaus Link, Prior of the Augustinian Eremites of Nuremberg and a celebrated preacher, the humanists had learned from Staupitz a blending of the theology of Augustine with later German mysticism characteristic of the Vicar-General. This prepared them for the deeper experimental teaching of Luther.

The glimpses we have had of the theology Staupitz used in his efforts to solve the problems of Luther show even better the blending of Augustine, Bernard, Tauler, humanism, and evangelicalism. Luther proved himself an apt pupil and Staupitz selected him to be his successor in the chair of Bible, for he knew Luther shared his enthusiasm for the Bible rather than dogmatic theology.

Many students attested to the influence of Staupitz as a teacher and theologian and acknowledged his worth and eminence. Of course, the pride of a relative is apt to be prejudiced, but the words of Nicholas Amsdorf, a nephew of Staupitz and close friend and devoted follower of Luther, are worth quoting. He was writing to Spalatin concerning some nuns who had escaped from a convent and gained refuge with Luther: "The oldest of these is the sister of my gracious lord and uncle, Dr. Staupitz. I have selected her, my dear brother, as your wife, that you may boast of your brother-in-law as I boast of my uncle." The influence of the man is again demonstrated by the historical note that Luther could not be touched by the machinery of his Order in Germany "because he stood so well with Staupitz. . . ."

One writer speaks of Staupitz as the "eminent predecessor" of Luther at the University of Wittenberg. Luther was first noticed not because of his own ability but because of the interest shown in him by the Vicar-General and Dean. Luther's own high regard for Staupitz prompted him to write to Spalatin in 1516, asking him to use his influence with the Elector to keep Staupitz from being made a bishop—as he was much too good for the position.

There are so few references to Staupitz after he left the University of Wittenberg that the picture becomes hazy. It is difficult to ascertain the date he stepped down officially from his position as Dean of the Theology Faculty; it is possible that he never did, officially. However, because of the constantly growing influence of Luther, it is assumed that when Luther came into prominence, the eminence of Staupitz faded. Staupitz, however, was quite closely connected with the fortunes of Luther until his retirement from the Vicariate in 1520.

It is interesting to see the various pulls on Staupitz as the years passed. He never did entirely forsake Luther, in spite of the fact that Luther accused him of doing so, and in spite of the fact he was not willing to go to the lengths to which Luther was willing to go. Nevertheless, his personal love and loyalty to Luther were not quite sufficient to offset the tug of loyalty to the Roman Church and subservience to the Church's authority.

When Staupitz brought Luther to Wittenberg he had a two-fold reason: to gain a brilliant mind for his faculty and to give that brilliant mind work that would be enhancing and engrossing. He could not foresee that the day would come when the young monk would change the world, but he did find that Luther had ideas that discomfitted his superiors.

It is common historical knowledge that the sale of indulgences was the immediate cause of the break-out of Luther, even though many before him were critical of the practice. In fact, one of the foremost critics of indulgences was Staupitz himself. In 1517, Luther wrote to the Vicar-General: "I remember, Reverend Father, having learned from you, as but a voice from heaven, that penance is not genuine unless it springs from a love of righteousness and God. Just when my heart was full of this thought, behold, new indulgences began to be proclaimed throughout the country in most noisy fashion." Again, Luther writes to Staupitz in March 1518, "Truly I have followed the theology of Tauler and of that book which you recently gave to Christian Döring to print; I teach that men should trust in nothing save in Jesus Christ only, not in their own prayers or merits or works, for we are not saved by our own exertions, but by the mercy of God." He was here referring to one of the books which Staupitz wrote, *On the Love of God*. His books, according to Luther and others, were quite popular, widely sold and read.

The loyalty of Staupitz to Luther in times of trouble and his influence on Luther's theology are well documented. But Luther was a loyal friend in return. In the years between the confessor-novitiate relationship and the posting of the Ninety-five Theses, Luther was not only a disciple of Staupitz but upheld him as well. On one occasion, Luther wrote to the Elector in defense of Dr. Staupitz, who was in disfavor at the time, quoting his own words as a means of restoring him to favor: "I [Staupitz] do not believe that I have ever done anything to displease my most gracious lord except to love him too much." Evidently this put him back in the Elector's good graces, for we later find the Prince taking a renewed interest in the welfare of the Vicar-General.

Luther not only interceded when there was a suggestion that Staupitz was to be made a bishop, he also did personal favors for his mentor. Once Luther wrote to one of the brothers who owed Staupitz some money: "We gave the two and half gulden you owe to the Reverend Father Vicar in your name; for the other half gulden you must either try to pay it or get him to remit the debt. For I feel that the Reverend Father was so well inclined to you that he would not object to doing so."

Luther was an advocate for Staupitz on other occasions. On June 30, 1516, he wrote to John Lang at Erfurt, counseling him to yield to those in charge there "because all of us, and I especially, are bound to uphold the honor of the Vicariate, and especially of the Reverend Father Vicar." On October 5 of the same year, Luther wrote again to Lang, mentioning that

Staupitz was forced to remain in Munich because of poverty, and remarking that he, Luther, wished to have Staupitz with him. In this year, Staupitz was sent by the Elector to secure relics for his collection, of which the Elector was inordinately proud. Staupitz was not having much success because he was vested with no authority to take whatever relics he discovered unless the owner permitted him to do so. In one instance in particular, he was refused by the Mother Superior of a convent, even though he presented his letter from the Elector. She professed to believe he might have "faked" the letter. In view of this situation, Luther wrote to his friend Spalatin to either get some authority for Staupitz, or else excuse him from the mission.

All this time Luther continued to seek the advice of Staupitz in regard to his teaching and his personal troubles, for his moods of depression never completely left him. Early in 1518, Luther was asked by his Augustinian brethren to go to Heidelberg to a chapter meeting and discuss theology. To this he readily agreed, because he had thought all along that he was only agreeing with true Catholic doctrine. He was received cordially by Staupitz and the rest of the Augustinian monks; they discussed his theology, with no charges brought or debated. Luther afterward said the cordial reception was an indication that he could not be a heretic.

Everything to this point shows a friendly relationship between the two men. Now, however, because of his position in the Order, Staupitz felt forced to take steps to quiet Luther as Luther's Reformation gained momentum. By the time of the Disputation with Eck at Leipzig, Luther was clearly on the same path as the condemned heretic, John Huss, who had been burned at the stake for his teachings. Eck immediately sought the most influential ears in Rome in his effort to silence Luther. Gabriel Volta, General of the Augustinian Order, wrote to Staupitz as Vicar-General of the Saxony Province, condemning Luther and charging him with heresy. Volta neglected to mention that on one point in the charge for which Luther was called to account by Rome—the condemnation of the Dominicans' endless repetition of prayers and psalms as mechanical—Staupitz himself was in complete agreement. Although Staupitz condemned Luther, as he was ordered to, it was in the name of Volta.

Staupitz wanted to have as little trouble as possible, as did the Bishop of Brandenburg, so they asked Luther to refrain from publishing for a while, which he did. Their efforts on his behalf appeared to be of little avail, however, and Luther, the incipient heretic, was summoned to Rome to answer the charges against him. But Luther well knew the danger in going to Rome, and refused to cooperate. In the late summer of 1518, the Emperor called a Diet to be held in Augsburg to settle problems of the Empire, including the case of Martin Luther.

Although Staupitz offered the Reformer sanctuary in Salzburg in case he did not want to risk going to Augsburg, Luther turned down the offer. Staupitz was not yet at the point where he would leave Luther, still believing his former pupil was correct in his position. Although he did not entirely approve of Luther's methods, Staupitz took issue only once with Luther's motives, and this was in his last letter to Martin, after he had made his peace with the Pope.

Staupitz went with Luther to Augsburg to face the Emperor and the Pope's representative, Cardinal Cajetan. Here Staupitz took his career and his life in his own hands by standing firmly with Luther. By orders from Rome, the Cardinal was free only to ask for recantation, not to dispute or to offer other solutions. When Cajetan could no longer contain himself and began to dispute with the accused heretic, Luther asked for the privilege of submitting his arguments in writing. The Cardinal at first refused, only conceding at the earnest request of Staupitz. Luther was ordered out of the presence of the Papal Legate, who realized later he should not have lost his temper.

On further reflection, Cajetan decided to make one more attempt to secure Luther's recantation. He sent for Staupitz and begged him to persuade Luther to recant, promising him that the monk should suffer no humiliation for doing so. To this end he prescribed a form of revocation which Staupitz presented, only to be told by Luther that he could not revoke against his conscience without express scriptural warrant. This the Vicar-General could not find. Ultimately, Luther deferred to the entreaties of Staupitz and Link, and wrote a humble letter to Pope Leo X, in which he admitted that in the heat of argument he had spoken indiscreetly, bitterly, and irreverently of the Pope. He also agreed to recant insofar as his conscience would permit, at the command and advice of the Vicar-General, although he could not do so merely on the grounds of arguments based on the views of Thomas Aquinas, the chief of scholastic theologians. Both Luther and Staupitz knew they were not giving in to the Pope or his emissaries, but they hoped to gain time and to salve the feelings of the Pope.

Gabriel Volta, general of the Augustinian Order in Rome, must have suspected what was happening at Augsburg, for he wrote to Hecker, leader of the Conventuals, about the failure of Staupitz to force the submission of Luther, asking him to use his influence in the matter. Staupitz and Luther were threatened with excommunication for their disobedience. Staupitz anticipated impending trouble. Rumor circulated that the Cardinal was contemplating the arrest of both Staupitz and Luther. Outwardly the Cardinal seemed friendly to them, calling Luther "my son," but, as Luther wrote to Carlstadt, "We don't trust the Italian further than we can see, for, perhaps, he is acting treacherously."

Nervous about his own safety and that of Luther, which he had guaranteed, Staupitz decided on a drastic step. He had tried to be a mediator and failed—though he had brought Luther as far toward submission as possible. Staupitz had done more than any other with the Wittenberg monk. Now, if the Cardinal demanded it, he would have to compel Luther, because of his vow of obedience, to recant, on pain of excommunication. This was a hard question for Staupitz to deal with. In the end he did what one would expect from a man of his character; in keeping with other decisive acts of his life, Staupitz formally absolved Luther from his vows as a monk, and sent for Link. The two of them left Augsburg secretly under cover of darkness.

The whole affair at Augsburg is best conveyed in the letter the Vicar-General sent to the Elector of Saxony on October 15, 1518, during the time of the Diet: "Serene, Highborn Prince, my most gracious Lord: The Legate from Rome acts as (alas) they all do there: he gives fair words, but all empty and vain. For his whole soul is bent on making Luther recant, not considering that Luther offers to stay still and debate publicly at Augsburg, and to give an answer and reason for this debate; yes, for every word in it. But the unjust judge does not want him to debate, but to recant. Nevertheless, Dr. Luther has in writing so answered his fundamental argument, that the Cardinal is straitened therein, and no longer trusts his own argument, but seeks here and there, this and that, how he may extirpate innocent blood and force recantation. God will be the just judge and protector of the truth. . . . He says also that there is in the land a letter of the General against Luther. Dr. Peutinger has heard it is also against me, with the purpose of throwing us in prison and using force against us. God be our guard! Finally I fear our Professor (Luther) must appeal and expect force. God help him! His enemies have become his judges; and those who sue him give judgment against him. Herewith I commend myself to your Grace and your Grace to the eternal God. I know nothing as yet certain to write. But if the affair shall take a more favorable turn I will write in haste to your Grace. Your Grace's humble, obedient chaplain, Dr. John von Staupitz." The deep faith of Staupitz, and his struggle to do what was right in the sight of God is well expressed here.

Although Luther wrote to Lang in the spring of 1519 complaining that Staupitz had forgotten him, he nevertheless consulted his superior before any action, such as later that same year when answering the charges of Eck. Luther refused to recognize several things. One was that Staupitz, in spite of the fact that Luther was classed as a heretic, offered him refuge before the Diet of Augsburg, saying in his letter, "Unless I make a mistake, the opinion prevails that no one should examine the Scripture without leave of the Pope in order to find out for himself, which Christ certainly commands us to do. You have few defenders, and would that they were not hiding for fear of enemies. I should like you to leave Wittenberg and come to me, that we may live and die together. This would also please the archbishop."

Luther also forgot that his old friend was being harried on every side by ecclesiastical superiors. The Emperor took the sudden departure of Staupitz very hard, thinking that the Vicar-General was trying to mock him. The Dominicans, always the rivals of the Augustinians, were constantly complaining to Staupitz about Luther and to the authorities at Rome when

Staupitz failed to force the submission of Luther. Although Staupitz was not named in the Bull of 1520, he suffered because of his known sympathies with Luther. Luther, in a letter to Spalatin, says that "without knowing it I have hitherto been teaching all that John Huss taught and so has Staupitz."

Later in 1520, Erasmus wrote an open letter in which he says, "A brave man was shown to Matthew Lang, Cardinal of Gurk at Cologne, commanding him to invite Staupitz, Vicar-General of the Augustinians, and force him to abjure all Luther's dogmas, and if he did not do this throw him in prison or punish him in some other way." Luther recognizes the danger to Staupitz in a letter to Spalatin in 1521: "The Pope has accused our Staupitz before the Cardinal of Salzburg for holding with me. Staupitz has answered; I know not whether he will be taken away."

Because of the constant troubles within the Order, and the evil days upon which the brotherhood had fallen, Staupitz resigned from the office of Vicar-General at the Eisleben Chapter meeting in 1520. But he was still able to influence the monks to be lenient with Luther through his successor Wenceslaus Link, a good friend of the Reformer.

But Staupitz would not follow Luther all the way. From Salzburg, where he retired to a Benedictine monastery, he sent a letter to the Pope in which he did not disclaim allegiance to the teachings of Luther but did declare complete submission to the Pope. This seemed to satisfy the Curia. Staupitz had hoped that retirement might bring him peace, but he was forced to write the letter to the Pope when the Pope called upon him to join in a condemnation of Luther's heresies. This so-called weakness of Staupitz grieved Luther very much, for he believed that submission to the Pope meant submission to all the doctrines of the Church.

It saddened Luther that Staupitz was so unwilling to go the whole way with him and that he had so weakened that he would write a conciliatory letter to the Pope. But Staupitz was well along in years now; rebellion is for younger men. Staupitz yearned for the peace which by his training and his life he could only expect from the Church. It was the natural thing for him to do—to leave the fight and watch his younger friend from a distance. He recognized in January 1521, in a letter to their mutual friend, Link, that his was not to be part of Luther's struggle in the storms ahead: "Martin has undertaken a hard task and acts with great courage illuminated by God; I stammer and am a child needing milk."

The thing that Luther could not see was that Staupitz was the high point in the Roman Church at its best, just as the Cardinal of Salzburg and the Pope were among the worst. He failed to recognize that no matter how deep the Church sank into a trough of moral and doctrinal lassitude, there would always be someone, some saving remnant of hope. In this case that remnant would be men like Staupitz and Luther himself. Because of Staupitz's wise and gentle piety, because of the view he had of the interpretation of the Scripture, and because he loved the Church, he was in accord with Augustine, Bernard, Francis, and the other great saints of the Church. In the same sense that they are called by one writer "Protestant Saints," Staupitz was a Protestant.

Perhaps John von Staupitz saw beyond Luther when he wrote in his last letter to Luther: "Greeting. You write me often, dear Martin, and suspect my constancy. To which I reply: My faith in Christ and the Gospel keeps me whole, even if I need prayer that Christ may help my unbelief, and that I may divorce all human interests and embrace the Church warmly. Spare me if, on account of the slowness of my mind, I do not grasp all of your ideas and so keep silent about them. . . . Alas, abuses creep into all things human, and there are few who measure all things from faith, but there are some, nevertheless, who do, and the substance of the thing is not to be condemned on account of some accidental evil that is found in it. . . . We owe you much, Martin, from having led us from the husks of swine back to the pastures of life and the words of salvation. . . . But the wind bloweth where it listeth; we owe you thanks for planting and watering, saving the glory of God, to whom alone we attribute the power of making sons of God. I have written enough. I wish that I could talk to you even one hour and open the secrets of the heart."

The letter ends with a paragraph that defines the life of Staupitz and his relationship with Luther, with a recognition of his essential oneness with the Reformer: "I commend to you, brother, the bearer of this letter, that you make him your disciple in industry and ability, and that he may receive the master's degree and so return to me. I hope he may bear good fruit to the honor of the University of Wittenberg in the future. I hope my unworthy request may prevail with you, as I was your precursor in the evangelical doctrine, and I still hate the Babylonian captivity. Farewell, and greet Melanchthon, Amsdorf, and my other friends."

CHAPTER 4

Philipp Melanchthon

Philipp Melanchthon's place in the pantheon of theologian/heroes is secure. He and Luther did not see eye to eye on all matters, and to the end of his life Melanchthon found it hard to accept a total break with Rome.

It is evident that Luther felt that Melanchthon was not as aggressively sure in his reform thinking and expression as he could or should have been. This may have been only a difference in temperament. Luther was confrontational—or at least always ready to be—while Melanchthon would avoid the shock approach whenever possible. One writer calls him the "Quiet Reformer." Another refers to him as Luther's "mild and moderate lieutenant" in a description of Melanchthon's part in drafting the Augsburg Confession, a move that pointed toward reconciling the views of Luther and Rome.

Timid and retiring he may have been, but Melanchthon's great scholarship and abilities in writing and organizing theological views were from the beginning of his time at Wittenberg at the command and service of Luther and the Reformation. In spite of the contrast in their personalities, they early became and continued as close friends through all the years to Luther's death, and Philipp Melanchthon gave the oration at Luther's funeral service at Wittenberg in 1546.

Like many scholars of the time and place, Philipp changed his name from Swarzerd, or "black earth," to its Greek equivalent, Melanchthon. Others of Luther's circle of friends and colleagues did the same, following a common practice among scholars of the day, especially those involved in Greek studies. Thus Juducus Koch became Justus Jonas, and John Bugenhagen was commonly called "Pomeranus," a recognition of his Pomeranian background.

Melanchthon was nearly fourteen years younger than Luther. He was born in Bretten, Baden, February 16, 1497, being a contemporary of Ferdinand and Isabella of Spain, Copernicus, and Erasmus, as well as Luther, Zwingli, Calvin, and other Reformation greats. His father, George Swarzerd, was an armorer, honored for his skill and craftsmanship. John Reuchlin, his father's uncle, was one of the great humanist scholars, frequently coupled with Erasmus, Colet, and More, as well as other bright stars of the Renaissance. It was Reuchlin who suggested to Philipp that his name be hellenized to Melanchthon. Luther on occasion pays his respects to the influence of Reuchlin, especially in his studies of Hebrew, Greek, and the New Testament. Philipp lived for a time with his grandmother, Reuchlin's sister, after his father died when he was only eleven years old. Barbara Reuter, his mother, also came from a respected family and was known as a woman of good sense. She is said to have been the author of some lines that were popular at the time:

Almsgiving beggareth not;
Church-going hindereth not;
To grace the ear delayeth not;
Gain ill-gotten helpeth not;
God's book deceiveth not.

Reuchlin lived in Pforzheim, where Philipp spent the years 1507–1509 attending Latin school. The boy then studied at the University of Heidelberg, where he earned a bachelor's degree in 1511. Then he went to Tübingen, where the master's degree was conferred in 1514. He was seventeen years old!

Reuchlin proposed his great-nephew, at the ripe old age of twenty-one, to the Elector Frederick, who had written to him in April 1518 asking him to recommend someone to teach Greek at his new University at Wittenberg. On July 24, the Elector wrote to Melanchthon, offering him the position. Leaving Tübingen without any expression of appreciation by his colleagues there, Philipp went to Wittenberg by a rather circuitous route, stopping at Augsburg to visit with the Elector and George Spalatin, the Elector's secretary. Evidently he was considered a fine "catch" for the Elector, for as he traveled, Bavarian leaders tried to persuade him to join the faculty at Ingolstadt, and later efforts were made to keep him at Leipzig for the faculty there. He had a friendly meeting with Williband Pirckheimer, one of the leading humanist scholars, as he passed through Nuremberg. In spite of his youth, he was already known for his scholarly accomplishments and promise. He arrived at Wittenberg the morning of August 25, 1518.

There was considerable surprise at his youthful and unimpressive appearance. Some wondered at the Elector bringing in a mere boy for so important a post. Others were surprised at

Reuchlin for recommending him, probably interpreting the recommendation as pure nepotism. Four days later, August 29, Melanchthon gave his first lecture, and doubts soon disappeared. Luther was so captivated that he wrote to Spalatin expressing appreciation for the "learned and elegant" lecture, and the "delight and admiration" of all the hearers. "If we can keep him, I wish no other teacher of Greek." In the middle of December, Luther wrote to Reuchlin, "Our Philipp Melanchthon is an admirable man; yea, there is hardly any respect in which he does not surpass other men; nevertheless he is on the best and most friendly terms with me." The bond between the soon-to-be-famous Luther and his younger colleague was forged quickly, never to be broken. Strained occasionally, yes; questioned sometimes, to be sure; but basically a sound, warm, friendship which came to include family members and University colleagues.

It is difficult to get a clear picture of individuals who lived and did their work almost five hundred years ago. But because so much has been researched and written about the German Reformation—and because the great artists Dürer and Cranach were close to the Reformers—we do have a rather good idea of the physical appearance of many of them. Melanchthon was frail and small, walked haltingly, and was evidently quite plain of features. The high forehead, hooked nose, thin face, scraggly beard, and piercing eyes stand out in Dürer's portrait, dated 1526. Luther, in a letter to Spalatin, refers to the "weakness of his outward appearance." Coupled with this rather terse description of his friend, Luther rejoices in and admires "that force that is in him." To Philipp's great uncle, Reuchlin, he writes about the same time that "Obviously, Melanchthon's appearance, however unprepossessing, was more than overcome by his mind," his thinking, and his doing.

There were differences between Luther and Menlanchthon, not only in physical being, but in temperament as well. Martin was unrestrained, as evidenced by his head-on collisions with the Church and its authorities; a man of action, he showed inflexibility in many situations, demanding immediate action. Philipp, on the other hand, was flexible; he could make room for contrary thought and opinion. Where Luther was unrestrained, Melanchthon showed restraint and caution and a mediating approach.

Melanchthon's debut at the University was followed by lectures on the classics: Hebrew, Latin, rhetoric, and philosophy. One writer reports that he had as many as 2000 in attendance on occasion—though one wonders if any hall in the University could accommodate such a crowd. Included among his listeners were not only students enrolled at the University, but townspeople and members of the nobility as well. Luther was stimulated by his younger colleague and directed students to Philipp's lectures, even those at six o'clock in the morning. Melanchthon combined his lecture schedule with extensive writing in the classics and in biblical subjects. Gradually he began to play a leading role in theological studies as well, and they became a major interest. However, Melanchthon was never ordained into the ministry of the Church.

Coming to Wittenberg as a teacher, Melanchthon never became a priest or pastor, even though Luther tried to move him in that direction. His mastery of Greek was a great help to Luther when the Reformer was engaged in translating the Bible. Philipp's teaching effectiveness and his concern for school reform and reorganization led to his being labeled as the "Preceptor of Germany." His continuing involvement with teaching kept Philipp in a cordial relationship with Erasmus, a relationship which Jonas, Spalatin, and others close to Luther, shared. Luther himself, however, after some early contacts with Erasmus, distanced himself from the humanist scholar, although he used Erasmus's Greek New Testament in his study and lectures.

In his Table Talk, Luther recognized at least the outlines of the differences in the thinking of the Reformers on a variety of subjects and that they differed from those outside the circle of Reformation leadership. On one occasion, he sat with friends, as was his custom at many meals, and wrote with chalk on the table: "Substance and words—Philipp. Words without substance —Erasmus. Substance without words—Luther. Neither substance nor words—Carlstadt." Melanchthon came in later and is reported to have said that Luther should be credited with words as well.

Not only did Melanchthon agree with Luther's thinking on secular subjects, they also agreed on the ideas and concepts that ultimately divided the Reformation and its leaders. Melanchthon was one of several humanists who were attracted to Luther. Beginning as Erasmian humanists, Martin Bucer, Huldrich Zwingli, Oecolampadius (John Hussgen), Melanchthon, and others, by 1519 were devoted to Luther's position, although Erasmus and Reuchlin, the most prominent of the humanists, did not become followers. As we know, Bucer, Zwingli, and Oecolampadius went another path.

Erasmus and Reuchlin, upon occasion, expressed publicly their affirmation of the justice of Luther's complaints about the Church, while retaining their nominal loyalty to Rome. When breaks came at different times in the Reformers' ranks, Melanchthon was always at the side of Luther, although sometimes some friction showed. It would probably be fair to say that Luther felt the friction more than did Melanchthon. In every major confrontation, though, Melanchthon stood with his friend and leader. Thus it is that Melanchthon sat beside Luther at Marburg, confronting Zwingli and Oecolampadius across the table, agreeing on all points but one: the interpretation of the Lord's Supper. The disagreement at this point marked the break between the German and the Swiss Reformers, a theological break that continues to the present. Melanchthon unsuccessfully tried to bridge the gap between the more radical Reformers, those who interpreted the Lord's Supper as "memorial," and the more conservative Reformers who insisted on the "real presence" of the true body and blood of Christ. This latter was the position of Luther, who wrote with chalk on the table at Marburg: "hoc est corpus meum"—this is my body.

While Luther distanced himself from the humanist leaders, he retained a friendly relationship with many whose scholarly outlook and religious understandings came out of or were conditioned by humanist influences. In correspondence with his intimate friends, such as Spalatin, Lang, and Melanchthon, he frequently signed his name "Eleutheris," which means "freedom" in Greek. It was later that Martin actually broke with the humanists, after his long-distance debate with Erasmus on free will. Philipp, whose early training was guided by his great-uncle Reuchlin, frequently gave evidence of his humanist background but never to the extent that he was separated from Luther in his expression or conclusions.

Luther and Melanchthon agreed in their conclusions of medieval scientific understanding. Copernicus was becoming known for his theory that the earth revolves around the sun and not the contrary. Luther, in rejecting the theory, wrote, "People give ear to an upstart astrologer who strove to show that the earth revolves, not the heavens or firmament, the sun and the moon . . . but the sacred Scripture tells us that Joshua commanded the sun to stand still, not the earth." About ten years later, Melanchthon received a copy of "The First Account of the Books of the Revolutions" (of celestial bodies) from a protégé, a young professor on the Wittenberg faculty, George Rheticus. He was not impressed, writing to a friend: "Some think it a distinguished achievement to construct such a crazy thing as that Prussian astronomer who moves the earth and firms the sun. Verily, wise rulers should tame the unrestraint of men's minds." Such discussions only indicate that Luther and Melanchthon were men of their time when they wandered into fields other than those of theology.

More than Luther, Melanchthon evinced an interest in astrology. In those days it was common to begin an investigation into any person's effectiveness by casting his horoscope. As astrologers still do, they began to look at the arrangement of the stars and planets on the date of birth. The figures of the zodiac, coming from ancient times, were representatives of the interpretations which followed, all being based on the idea that the stars and planets had an influence on individuals which could be established and charted. Records indicate that Melanchthon cast the horoscope of Luther several times. This interest was shared with many of the eminent scholars of the time, and Melanchthon made decisions for himself, his family, and the University on the basis of astrological determinations. Upon occasion, he made public speeches defending astrology as a science, including a kind of scriptural support in that the firmament is a part of God's creation, and that to fail to study this, with the movement of the stars and the planets, would be to fail to know God's purposes.

Angels and demons also were a part of the theological and social and political matrix of the period. The longtime tradition that Luther hurled an ink-pot at the devil while in the Wartburg fits into his and Melanchthon's thinking in such matters. Good and evil were personified by real figures. Once Philipp warned his students about bathing in the Elbe River because of the danger of being attacked by evil spirits. Evil omens were common and well-heeded. Luther's and Melanchthon's thinking was typical of the times, and they were prime examples that men of the highest education and intellect were as prone to such concepts as the illiterate peasant—only sounding more learned as they justified their positions.

Through his extravagant success as a lecturer and writer, Philipp was drawn closer and closer to Luther, as Luther was to him. Almost a year and a half after the posting of the Ninety-five Theses, Melanchthon was one of those who accompanied Luther to Leipzig for the debate with John Eck. Philipp did not enter into the debate but served as a resource person for the Wittenberg party, offering arguments and facts. He referred to himself as an "idle spectator," but evidently was so active a participant that Eck felt it necessary to make public a reply to Melanchthon's criticisms some eleven days after the disputation closed. To this reply, Philipp made a rather lengthy response, placing himself firmly on the side of Luther, eschewing scholasticism, basing his position on the Bible.

As he thus began his open participation in the Reformation Movement, Melachthon recognized that he was more than ever before a "Lutheran." His and Luther's lives drew closer together. Within half a dozen years they both would be married; their families would be close; with their friends and colleagues they would be the de facto leaders of a movement that changed the religious and social and political life of Germany and their world.

We identify the early stirrings of the Reformation with Luther's proposition that we are "justified by faith," and his defiant statement at Worms that his warrant is in the Scriptures, to which every person shall have access. Melanchthon, in 1519, seeking his Baccalaureate in theology, placed on the University bulletin board his own twenty-four theses, or statements he would defend. They were aimed at the doctrine of justification by faith as being accredited by Scripture. The twenty-four statements included rejection of transubstantiation of the bread and wine of the Mass as being scripturally without foundation.

Eck saw Philipp's statements as a weapon aimed at the whole basic concept of the priestly function of the Church of Rome. Luther also understood how far Melanchthon had gone in a new direction, one he himself was favoring. To Staupitz he confided in a letter, "You have seen, or will see, Philipp's theses . . . they are bold, but they are certainly true."

Everyone close to the Reform Movement was aware not only of the differences in thought and action between Luther and Melanchthon, but also of the bond of friendship that held them together. Certainly the two leaders were also aware of this. On one occasion Luther wrote to a friend, "I can cut through a willow branch with a knife, but to cut through oak requires an axe and a wedge, and even with these one can hardly split it . . . Philipp stabs, too, but only with pins and needles. . . . But when I stab, I do it with a heavy pike of the sort used for hunting boars." Philipp understood this, and stayed loyal because he knew the great value of the things of which Luther was capable.

Which is not to say that Melanchthon could not, upon occasion, be as stubborn and forceful an adversary as Luther. He joined Luther in bouts against the Anabaptists, especially in Saxony and Thuringia. He thought of them as corrupters of the faith, since they appeared to hold a doctrine of salvation by works and the law, rather than faith alone. Because of the close connection between religion and government, they were, in his eyes, political and social heretics as well.

As the Peasants Revolt unfolded in 1524–1525, the peasants were given both direction and push by Thomas Müntzer and Andrew Carlstadt. While Carlstadt did not call for bloody revolt, Müntzer did, claiming visions, and declaring that revelations to him were a better guide than Scripture. Luther, Melanchthon, and others of the Wittenberg Reformers were slow to realize the extent of the revolt in terms of property damage, personal assaults, and a general defiance of authority. While one would perhaps have expected Luther's reaction to be combative—he wrote a tract saying that the peasants should be hunted down and destroyed, and that the princes should "stab, smite, and strangle them"—Melanchthon penned a parallel tract in "confutation of the articles of the peasants" in which he went along with Luther's prescription that the princes were the ones to deal with the peasants, punishing them, however brutally.

At the Battle of Frankenhausen, May 15, 1525, Müntzer was captured and put to death. After much torture, his head was put on a stake to set an example. Luther and Melanchthon were regretful that he had only been tortured once. Melanchthon said he was sorry that Müntzer had not been forced to confess that he was doing the bidding of the devil. Gentle Philipp!

As the Reformation grew in influence and acceptance, Luther called upon Philipp to carry out a number of assignments. Such requests continued to the death of Luther and frequently led Melanchthon to express ideas and positions that were somewhat distant and variant from Luther's. On a variety of subjects Philipp moved away from Luther's rigid and uncompromising attitudes. Thus, Melanchthon softened Luther's position as he developed the Code of Instructions for Inspectors of Parsonages. He went further and urged the retention of many festivals and holy days. He said that, while it was right that people should partake of both elements at the Lord's

Supper, there were some "weaker brethren" who could not conscientiously receive communion in both kinds, and they should be allowed to continue receiving only one element as they gradually moved into the new order of things.

The fact that Melanchthon modified Luther's positions does not mean that he and Luther were in conflict in the sense that there was real friction or a breakdown in communication and relationship. Far from it. Their relationship continued to grow in warmth and respect over the years. Frequently Luther moved toward Melanchthon's point of view in political, theological, and organizational matters. They complemented each other. And all the while, as Luther puts it, he and Philipp and Amsdorf may have been drinking Wittenberg beer while the Word was at work—a quick reminder of the close relationship being sustained—while theological and political worlds were being shaken. While Melanchthon was at least a closet humanist, his close relationship with Luther conditioned his thinking. So, while he had great respect and collegial admiration for Erasmus and the humanist approach to affairs of church and state, his primary point of reference was the Scriptures.

Melanchthon's *Loci Communes*, first prepared in 1521 but revised and edited in printings over the next twenty years, demonstrated that Melanchthon and Luther agreed theologically from the very beginning of their friendship. Though he began as a humanist, Philipp had so thoroughly accepted Luther's theological concept of "faith alone" that he became the spokesman for the German Reformation. Many others also provided theological expression as the Reformation grew and spread, but the basic formulations were those laid out by Melanchthon. Luther frequently said that Philipp surpassed him in theology and regretted that he could not persuade

Philipp to preach, since he would then be able to carry the theology of the Reformation to the people.

In *Loci Communes*, Melanchthon considered sin, grace, and law from the standpoint of the Lutheran proposal that Scriptures, not councils of Fathers of the Church, and faith alone—*sola fide*—not works, provided the proper theological stance for the believer. The book has been called the "first systematic statement of the Protestant Theology" and is based on Melanchthon's early lectures on the Letter to the Romans, a series which he gave at the insistence of Luther. By 1525, some eighteen editions had been published in Latin, plus a German edition translated by Spalatin. Justus Jonas, another of the inner circle of Luther's friends and colleagues, also provided a translation into German, with Philipp publishing his own German version later on. *Loci Communes* was considered one of the primary texts of the German Reformation and continued to be used for many years after the death of Melanchthon.

In later editions, changes and additions were made that gave the book a pronounced humanist flavor. There was no separation from Luther's main thesis of scriptural grounding for the doctrine of justification by faith. And Luther did not feel that Philipp was betraying the movement or their mutual understanding of it. While there is increasing evidence in succeeding editions of the humanist methodology, it is clear that Luther moved closer to Melanchthon's position than did Melanchthon to Luther's. The Reformer moved toward a softer view of predestination and a more moderate position on the real presence in the Lord's Supper—a softening that dulled some of the rigidities of his thinking about the dualism between reason and revelation, natural and revealed truth as the grounding of the Christian faith.

Philipp Melanchthon, in monument to Luther at Worms.

The two leaders were again collaborators when the Elector Frederick called upon them to do something about reports which came to him from unlettered, misfit, and malcontent priests and monks. Some of the malcontents had left the Roman Church without any real understanding of Reformation theology or practice. Their schools were badly handled, and their lives were no real model for their constituents, with marriage, divorce, salaries and other concerns contributing to a lack of ethical concern. Visitors were sent out by the Elector, with instructions from Luther and Melanchthon. Philipp, along with

Frederick Myconius, Justus Menius, Jerome Schurf, John von Paniz, and Erasmus von Haugwitz comprised the Commission to visit in Thuringia. They were appalled at the conditions they found. Other Commissions, there were five of them altogether, found the same deplorable situations in other areas.

Out of his experiences with the Visitation Commissions Melanchthon prepared a manual of guidance for future commissions in 1527. The guide consisted of two parts, the first being a statement of faith in Reformation terms and the second a specific plan for the operation of schools. This was the first confession of faith for the Reformers and the beginning of a thoroughgoing approach to general education. After further visitations by Melanchthon and Luther the following year, many of the churches and schools were reorganized, following the precepts of the Visitation Articles, as they were called. The two leaders provided catechisms for education in the faith and helped the sometimes incompetent pastors by writing sermons. This was all at the behest of the Elector, who received optimistic reports from Luther after a couple of years.

The articles also became important in the growing organizational structure of the Reformation churches. Most of the first part of the Visitation Articles were concerned with doctrine and proposed instruction of pastors in such matters as worship grounded in the basics of the Reformation: justification by faith, and the sole authority of Scripture. Melanchthon arranged for the printing of the articles, and they were presented to each of the pastors.

Sickness, sometimes quite serious, struck the two Reformers from time to time, and they shared a deep concern for one another. Medical treatment was quite primitive by our standards, with potions and folk remedies predominating. After Melanchthon had participated in the arrangement of the bigamous marriage of Philip of Hesse to Margaret in 1540, he was struck by a dangerous illness.

Messengers sped to Luther and Cruciger in Wittenberg, carrying the news that Melanchthon was dying and urging them to come as quickly as possible. When Luther arrived, one who was there said that Melanchthon's understanding was almost gone, his eyes were dim, he could hardly speak, he knew no one, and could neither eat nor drink. Luther importuned God in prayer, indicating that not only he, Luther, was concerned, but that God should share in that concern. Martin said that he "wearied God's ears," reminding him of "all his promises of hearing prayers." Then he took the hand of Melanchthon, and, speaking gently, told him that "God takes his pleasure in life, not in death," that God still had work for him to do. Melanchthon asked to be let alone to die, but Luther asked for some soup to be brought and insisted that Philipp eat it, under threat of being excommunicated.

The caring concern of his friends, the threat of excommunication—which Philipp evidently took seriously—and the soup, apparently were effective. Philipp rallied and began a slow recovery. Later he wrote to his friend, Camerarius, "I cannot possibly describe to you the terrible pangs I suffered during my illness . . . I could see Luther was in agony of mind. . . . If he had not come to me, I would have died." Martin wrote to his wife, Katie, telling her that he was "gorging like a Bohemian, and swilling like a German. . . . The reason is that Master Philipp was truly dead, and he has risen from the dead just like Lazarus." Both Philipp and Martin saw in the experience the evidence of the power of prayer and the closeness of their relationship in every endeavor. Philipp, in later years, called it one of the major experiences of his life, quoting from Psalm 118: "I shall not die, but live and declare the works of the Lord."

The closeness of the two men was seen again and again as they discussed the implications of their theology. All of the Reformers taught that in the matters of righteousness and salvation, the will was subordinate to God's grace. Everything was a direct gift from God, not dependent upon themselves. They did not earn; God bestowed. This was basic, of course, to all of Luther's training and writing. Yet at this important point, Melanchthon was not completely at one with Luther, and Luther knew it and never quarreled with him about it. It was the humane element in humanism that moved Philipp to modify his own thinking toward a more Erasmian approach. Officially he never left the side of Luther, but there were many instances in which he was more conciliatory than his leader, especially, for example, as he developed the Augsburg Confession and other documents intended to soften the break with Rome.

In a sense, Melanchthon was carrying water on both shoulders, maintaining his support of and adherence to Luther and at the same time always seeming to leave a door open—to Zwingli and the Swiss Reformers, and to the humanists and to the Catholic theologians as well. At the deferred Diet of Speyer in 1529, the Emperor's position—that "evil, grave, perilous, and pernicious doctrine and errors" on the part of Evangelicals posed a threat to the empire—was supported by a narrow margin by the assembled princes and prelates. This reestablished the worst effects of the Edict of Worms (1521) which had condemned Luther and any who were foolish enough and brave enough to follow him. Melanchthon, who had been chosen, along with Agricola, by the Elector John to be at his side during the Diet, seems to have gone to Speyer with the idea of seeking peace in the Church.

One outcome of the Diet of 1529 was the definition of the Reform Movement as "Protestant," a move which Melanchthon saw as necessary. Reacting to the narrowly voted action to revert to the Edict of Worms, placing Luther and his followers in the position of heretics and blasphemers subject to persecution and punishment, six princes and fourteen cities formally "protested" the vote, claiming freedom of conscience and the rights of minorities. King Ferdinand, who presided in the absence of the Emperor, refused to acknowledge the protest. After adjournment of the Diet, the protest was sent by the evangelical party to the Emperor. The messengers were apprehended and put in prison. Through all this maneuvering, Philipp did as he had on many occasions, holding to a conciliatory position until he found it to be untenable, and then becoming just as aggressive as Luther in supporting the Reform position.

Later in 1529, at Marburg, as the German Reformers debated the fundamental assumptions of the movement with their Swiss counterparts, Melanchthon went through the same process. He began with the avowed intent of finding common ground and ended with a strong acceptance of Luther's hard-nosed approach. Even though he confessed to struggling with the problem, he joined Luther in refusing even to shake hands with Zwingli, accepting Luther's dictum, "Yours is a different spirit from ours." This only reiterated what Luther had written a year or so earlier in 1528, "I do not regard Zwingli as a Christian, for he holds and teaches no part of the Christian faith correctly, and has become sevenfold worse than when he was a papist."

In 1530, Emperor Charles V, having reached a time of comparative calm, called a Diet in Augsburg to seek answers to religious questions. Luther specifically was not allowed to attend, but Melanchthon was on hand to represent the evangelical position. He was called upon to do so after the German princes had risked their fiefdoms and their lives by refusing to kneel for the blessing of Cardinal Campeggio. Then, John of Saxony, Luther's prince, led the way into the Cathedral, where all knelt at the high altar—all, that is, except John of Saxony himself, and Philip, Landgrave of Hesse. They remained standing. The following day the Emperor called them in and told them their pastors could not preach in Augsburg. The princes resisted the Emperor at every point, even when the Emperor commanded that the evangelical pastors should not preach polemical sermons that might cause trouble. Then he commanded that they march in the Corpus Christi parade the next day. They refused.

When the Emperor continued to insist, the elderly Margrave George, of Brandenburg, said, "Before I let anyone take from me the Word of God and ask me to deny my God, I will kneel and let him strike off my head." The Emperor, just reaching his thirtieth year, unable to find a response to a declaration of this kind from one of his oldest and most respected princes, said in his poor German, "Not cut head. Not cut head." These were brave men! At this point, Melanchthon was called upon to prepare a confessional statement. He was apparently hopeful that the break with the Emperor and those more moderate in the Church could be healed. He had no desire to deny Luther's position, but he felt strongly that he did not want to be one of those who would destroy the Church. At one point he said that the real difference between the Catholics and the followers of Luther was nothing more than the use of German in the Mass.

Luther, sitting out the Diet of Augsburg at Coburg, wrote to Philipp that he was willing to be conciliatory in personal matters but not willing to be as conciliatory as his friend in public controversy. Melanchthon had not been willing to make gestures of conciliation at Marburg, yet now he was seemingly willing to recognize the Pope, while Luther was advocating eliminating papal functions entirely. To Luther, Melanchthon seemed to be willing to give up on the major premises of the Reformation.

This was not the case in the end. The Augsburg Confession which Melanchthon prepared was quiet in tone, yet quite solid in its adherence to the faith of Luther. It was in keeping with the obstinate faith expressed by the princes in their refusal to kneel before the Cardinal at the high altar. Melanchthon's first draft represented electoral Saxony, but in its final form it spoke for all of Luther's followers. The Diet was convened to find some settlement of the religious problems in the empire, including not only the Germans but also the Swiss Reformers and those following the Strassburgers. The Swiss leaders were not satisfied with the statement on the Eucharist, refusing to sign Melanchthon's confession, preferring to offer their own statement, as did the Strassburg Reformers. Thus, there were three confessions, or statements of faith, with the Anabaptists not being recognized in any of the three.

The Augsburg Confession was read in public for the first time on June 25, 1530. The Emperor listened and then gave the Evangelicals until April 1531 to submit to the Church and the imperial will, with the threat of military force, arrest, and punishment if they did not submit. Even in the face of such a threat, Luther sought for moderation on the part of the Church and the Emperor through his one-time friend, Albert, Archbishop of Mainz. His appeal began with a frank admission: "Inasmuch as there is no hope of unanimity in the faith," and went on to propose that the Catholic leaders keep the peace, allowing all to believe the truth as they understood it, and suggesting that God never forced anyone to believe. Actually, there was a kind of peace for some fifteen years, largely because the Emperor was busy on other fronts.

The Augsburg Confession was and still is a basic doctrinal statement of the Lutheran denominational churches. When it was adopted by the Reformation leadership, Melanchthon thought he had made it too strong in tone, even though his first thought was that it was too mild in its effort at reconciliation. The Catholic response was a Confutation, written by Eck, Faber, Cochleus and others, so violent in its tone that the Emperor rejected it. In rewriting, the Confutation was more judicious in approach and was read publicly with the Confession on August 3. To the demand of the Emperor that the Lutherans accept the teachings of the Church and the authority of the Pope, Melanchthon replied with Luther-like bravery, "We cannot yield, or desert the truth. We pray that for God's sake and Christ's that our opponents will grant us that which we cannot surrender with a good conscience." Later in the year, Melanchthon prepared an Apologia for the Confession, in answer to the Confutation, although his only knowledge of the latter was based on hearsay from those who heard it read. It did not see print until much later, 1579.

A rift between Luther and Melanchthon threatened during the period of the Diet of Augsburg as a result of Melanchthon carrying on a private negotiation with the Papal Legate, Campeggio. He wrote on July 6, "We have no doctrine that divides us from the Roman Church, and we are ready to obey it, if it will leave us a free course . . . if the Pope would not condemn us, unification might easily be accomplished." The Nurembergers, who became aware of this, thought Philipp was being childish and declared, "At this Diet, there is no man until now that has caused the Gospel more shame than Philipp." Fortunately, Luther did not agree with those critical of Philipp, recognizing that his friend was saying what he himself had said upon occasion, even though he had now moved beyond such expressions.

Melanchthon realized that Luther was not a creative theologian, rather that he clarified and made vital the doctrines of penance, forgiveness of sins, faith, and the importance of the Cross. He saw that Luther's primary emphasis was on grace as opposed to law and the fundamental distinction between the gospel and philosophy. By philosophy, Melanchthon meant the speculative studies which demanded a degree of detachment and objectivity.

Luther joined Melanchthon and other scholastics in the use of disputation as a means to truth. When he was engaged in disputation, however, he depended upon eloquence of delivery, colorful and memorable phrases, and frequently, heavy irony. Luther said, "I have a small voice." His friend said, "Nevertheless, it carries well." Luther said "I was born to go to war and give battle to sects and devils. That is why my books are stormy and warlike. . . . But Master Philipp comes softly and neatly, tills and plants, sows and waters with pleasure, as God has abundantly given him the talents."

Luther apparently did not intend to be, nor think of himself as, a speculative thinker. He did not intend to say anything original. His effort was to understand Scripture and make its meaning as clear as humanly possible. His thinking was exegetical as opposed to the didactical analyses of Melanchthon. Which is not to say that Philipp did not accept the primacy of Scripture but that the two men looked at Scripture through different eyes.

Luther reached the hearts of common people as did no other; Melanchthon commanded intellectual respect as no other man. Luther was frequently rough, sometimes uncouth, sometimes unwise, tough and impulsive; Melanchthon was rather timid, irresolute, with a tendency to compromise. They were devoted friends, who shared their friendship with the inner circle: Jonas, Bugenhagen, Spalatin, and their families and colleagues.

Martin was thirty-four when he posted the Ninety-five Theses on the Castle Church door at Wittenberg; Philipp was just twenty. In spite of the difference in age, there was a mutual attraction, with the older man treating the younger not only as an equal, but as his superior in ability and potential. From the outset they talked together; wrote letters to each other when they were apart; debated with each other; supported each other in every conflict, even though they didn't agree at every point; were concerned about each others' families; and spent leisure time together. In all these ways they were close, if not "closer than brothers." One who understands this has a better chance of understanding Martin Luther.

When Luther traveled to the first Diet of Augsburg in 1518 in fear of his life, he wrote to Melanchthon: "Play the man and teach the students the things that are right. I go now, if it is God's will, to be slaughtered as a sacrifice for you and for them. I prefer death to recantation, even if it means—and this would be my greatest sorrow—to lose your blessed society forever."

In 1520, when Karl von Miltitz, Papal Nuncio, tried to heal the breach between Rome and the Reformers at Wittenberg, a meeting was arranged at Lichtenberg where Melanchthon accompanied Luther, along with other Augustinians. This was among the first instances in which friendship and mutual respect between the two men brought them together in defense and dissemination of Luther's propositions.

That same year, Luther concluded that two things would improve Melanchthon's health, always precarious at best. One was an increase in salary, the other was for Philipp to find a wife. The first of these concerns was satisfied after some delays by appeals to the Elector through his secretary, George Spalatin. The second came quite soon after a brief courtship of Katherine, daughter of the Mayor of Wittenberg, Hieronimus Krapp. Philipp submitted to his friends' matchmaking with a typical scriptural word, "for the sake of the Gospel." However, his approach seems to have been properly romantic: "She has the qualities I could expect only from the immortal gods." Among those present at the wedding were Luther's two sisters, his father, and mother. Happily, the Elector not only sent some wild game and wine for the wedding celebration, but word that Philipp would have a raise in salary.

Philipp and Katherine had four children who often played with the children of Luther and Jonas and were frequently mentioned in the continuing correspondence of the Reformers when they were separated. The affection and concern in which they held one another and their children was evident in the letter which Luther wrote to Jonas several weeks after the death of Philipp's two-year-old son: "Philipp is still grieving. We all sympathize with him." The joy of the children playing together, the problems in rearing them, the pleasure the parents had in the relationship, were all touched upon in conversation and correspondence. The families were as close in their friendship as the fathers in their collaboration in the Reform Movement, an intimate relationship that was sustained over many years.

When Melanchthon was only twenty-two, Luther took him along to Leipzig for the Disputation with Eck. At Leipzig Luther confessed that upon occasion he gave up his own judgment in favor of that of Philipp because, "I venerate the work of God in him."

Philipp was not among those who went with Luther to Worms in 1521. The Elector Frederick had secured a safe-conduct for Luther, but any who accompanied him did so at their own peril. Feeling that he could be going to his death, Luther wrote to Philipp: "If I do not return, and my enemies should kill me at Worms, as may very well come to pass, I adjure you, dear brother, not to neglect teaching, nor fail to stand by the truth. In the meantime also do my work, because I cannot be there. You can do it better than I can. The Lord still finds a worthy champion in you." Melanchthon did not see Luther again for a number of months, not knowing for some time whether he was alive or dead, the kidnapping and safe-keeping at the Wartburg being so secretly accomplished. Philipp, along with many others, believed that Luther had been killed.

Believing the worst about Luther's disappearance, Melanchthon entered into a spirited defense of his leader, writing an "Apology by Philipp Melanchthon for Luther." The Reformer was given a copy and rejoiced in it. Needless to say, Philipp was overjoyed when he learned the true circumstances of the kidnapping and Luther returned to Wittenberg, where Melanchthon became a close collaborator in his translation of the Scriptures. Melanchthon's expertise in Greek, and that of Aurogallus in Hebrew, provided the scholarly assistance that made the project a successful venture.

Although Philipp had not gone with Luther to Worms, he too was in the danger since he publicly and privately supported the Reformer. He was the one who, shortly after his wedding, posted on the door of the City Church in Wittenberg a notice to the undergraduates of the University that he proposed to burn the "impious" books of papal law and Catholic theology. This bonfire was the one onto which Luther threw the Bull of Excommunication which had been issued against him.

While Luther was at the Wartburg in September 1521, Melanchthon accepted his statement that "the words of the canon are plain: let the canon yield to the Gospel." Thus began one of the most public demonstrations of the meaning of reform—administering communion to some students in the parish church in both bread and wine. And Melanchthon was not ordained!

So, as they moved from burning Papal Bulls to debate and confrontation with religious and political authorities, the two were together, for better or for worse, in sickness and in health. Philipp did have questions about why he was not invited to Martin's wedding, but apparently it caused no schism between the two men. Martin's forceful energy, coupled with Philipp's intellectual and philosophical resources, provided a strong leadership for the movement that changed the political and economic, the educational and religious face of Germany and Europe.

Even when indefensible actions and decisions occurred, such as the Peasant's War, the vituperation directed at their opponents by both of them, and the bigamy of Philip of Hesse in 1540, Luther and Melanchthon were, in every sense, hand in hand. Philipp evidently disliked and disapproved of the rough side of Martin, yet he continued to have a real and deep affection for him.

When Luther became ill at Leipzig in 1545, the University of Wittenberg sent Melanchthon, Bugenhagen, the Mayor of Wittenberg, and the Elector's personal physician to take care of him. The next year Luther went from Wittenberg to try to resolve the differences between the Counts of Mansfeld, accompanied by his sons, Martin and Paul. At Halle, his friend Jonas joined him and they went to Eisleben, Luther's place of birth, where they stayed until the matter of the Counts was settled in a friendly manner. In addition, Luther preached and took part in services of communion and ordination.

In a frail condition, Martin became ill, suffered apparent heart attacks, and died the night of February 18, 1546. His body was taken to Wittenberg for burial, below the pulpit in the Castle Church. Bugenhagen preached, and Melanchthon gave a Latin oration at the funeral service. Philipp, who died fourteen years later, was also buried in the Castle Church and lies close to his friend.

There is little question that Melanchthon came under the spell of Luther from the first, a spell he never tried to cast off. He ranked his friend Martin with the great characters of the Bible—Isaiah, John the Baptist, Paul—and the great doctors of the Church, such as Augustine. He said, "I would rather die than be separated from this man." And Luther reciprocated, frequently praising and commending Melanchthon as one "who excels all the doctors in the arts and true philosophy."

One biographer quotes Luther, comparing his approach to life and Malanchthon's: "I am rough, boisterous, stormy and altogether warlike. I am born to fight against innumerable monsters and devils. I must remove stumps and stones, cut away thistles and thorns, and clear the wild forests; but Master Philipp comes along softly and gently, sowing and watering with joy, according to the gifts which God has abundantly bestowed upon him." From such mutual understanding and appreciation, Martin Luther and Philipp Melanchthon forged the leadership of the Reformation in Germany.

CHAPTER 5

John Bugenhagen

hen one is given a nickname, it is usually meant either as a term of derision and disparagement or a token of affection. Sometimes Luther and the Wittenbergers called the pastor of the City Church "Dr. Bugenhagen." More frequently he was "Dr. Pomeranus," or merely "Pomeranus." This affectionate designation given to John Bugenhagen reflected his Pomeranian origin, sometimes being shortened to "Pomer," or even merely "Pom." To Luther and the group that made the Reformation the force it was in the Germany of the sixteenth century, the nickname was a friendly reference to a powerful preacher and administrator, one who contributed greatly to the movement, and perhaps more than any other to the reformation of the Mass.

Christened Johann Bugenhagen, he was born in Wollin, a Pomeranian town in northern Germany, June 24, 1485. After an early education in the local schools, he went to the University of Greifswald. As was the case with many of the leaders of the

Reformation, he was educated for the priesthood, entering the Augustinian Order. He was ordained a priest in 1509. Bugenhagen was teaching in Treptow when he became Vicar of the town church. His loyalty to Rome was complete, and he never dreamed that he would someday be in the thick of the battle called the Reformation.

His Order was that of the Praemonstratenses, a group that followed the Rule of Augustine, but went beyond the rule to a life of much greater austerity. In England they were called the "White Canons" from the color of their habit, which in turn was perhaps a symbol of the purity of life which they were to exemplify. They were not monks, but canons regular, and their work was that of preaching and the pastoral office. The training of Bugenhagen in this Order eminently fitted him for the part he was eventually to play: that of organizer and practical churchman in the Reformation. His studies of theology were extensive, and, next to Melanchthon and Luther, he was known as a theologian of great ability.

Bugenhagen left his teaching and preaching position in Treptow in 1517 for a position as head of the monastic school at Belbuck, where he also lectured on the Bible and the Church Fathers. In 1520, he read Martin Luther's *On the Babylonian Captivity of the Church*. This was not the first time he had heard of the Wittenberg monk, who had displeased him greatly by his attacks on indulgences.

Bugenhagen shared the sense of revulsion that was felt by many orthodox churchmen in reading Luther's tract. Later he said that he threw it away "like a live coal," although he had been attracted by Luther's other tracts. By the time he left Belbuck, he had re-read the tract, had discussed it with others, had given it greater thought, and had become a true believer.

Bugenhagen's conversion to the evangelical position and to Luther was a curious parallel to that of St. Paul. He was studying the treatise for the purpose of refuting it, and the study so changed him that he felt that "the whole world may be wrong; but Luther is right." In this judgment, he echoed what many others concluded, when, after reading and re-reading the Reformer's work, they moved from being critics to being followers. He proved that his was a true and moving conversion by winning over his Prior and most of his companions and became the Reformer of the Pomeranians. If Luther had had such startling results from every young theologian who heard him or read his works, the Reformation would have been a much simpler affair.

Because of his intense, if somewhat abrupt, interest in Luther, Bugenhagen could not have been but pleased and happy when his friend, Peter Suaven, invited him to Wittenberg to study. His reputation as a lecturer had preceded him. Without an official appointment, he was in 1521 engaged as a lecturer in his new location. He had scarcely had time to get settled in Wittenberg when he made a prediction that reverberated through his own personal experience. The question had been raised whether monks who were leaving the monasteries should be forced to return or be allowed to marry. Luther had searched the Scriptures, came to conclusions, and wrote theses on monastic vows, with special reference to celibacy and marriage. With Suaven, Bugenhagen was dining at the home of Melanchthon when the first of Luther's series of theses on monastic vows arrived from the Wartburg. "These theses," said Bugenhagen, "will affect a revolution in the existing order."

Always zealous in his work with the Reformer, the Pomeranian was one of the first to apply Luther's most recent theses to his own life. He just may have been waiting for someone to give moral support to his ideas. A little over a year after making the dinner-table statement, he married "an honest Wittenberg girl." This characterization of Bugenhagen's wife was given by Felix Ulscenius in a letter to Wolfgang Capito, the Strassburg Reformer, in July 1522. Although Felix speaks of the marriage of Bugenhagen, he is probably referring to the betrothal, for the actual wedding was not until October of that year.

One wonders how Dr. Pomeranus was able to support his young bride, since all the Augustinians were notoriously poor, including even such well-knowns as Staupitz and Luther. Lecturing was fine as a means of expression and developing the theology of the Reformation, but it was no means of practical support. Before the marriage of Bugenhagen, Luther had written to Spalatin in an effort to gain from the Elector, who seems to have footed all the bills for the University, a paying job for the lecturer: "It remains for you to accept the task of securing from the Elector for John Bugenhagen, one of those stipends that have heretofore been thrown away on the sophists. For next to Philipp (Melanchthon) he is the best professor of theology in the world. I fear, nay, I know, that there is danger that he may be carried off to Erfurt, and I wish him to be kept here; who knows how long I shall be allowed to stay?"

We may well speculate on the value Bugenhagen gave to this request of Luther when he was making plans for an October wedding. While this was a wonderful recommendation for the newest addition to the teaching staff, it evidently didn't buy bread for the bride, for within four months after the wedding, Luther was forced to write another prodding letter to Spalatin, this in January 1523: "I could not conceal from you that it has hitherto been the pride of our University that the lectures were given gratis by the bounty of the Elector. But now, Bugenhagen, out of dire necessity, lessens this reputation by the lectures he is giving, for he cannot teach for nothing, and yet his students think it a hardship to have to pay, but they are not willing to do without. Meanwhile, those who receive stipends are either not lecturing at all, or else they are men who are not to be compared with Bugenhagen in any respect. Mention this to the Elector, then, when you can; perhaps he may be willing to remedy the matter. Although the lectures of Philipp and Carlstadt are excellent and there are enough of them, nevertheless I would not be without those of Bugenhagen . . . I tell you this in confidence."

Whether or not Bugenhagen received any immediate results from the letters of Luther, we do not know. However, he was able to support his wife, for in 1523 he became pastor of the City Church, and in 1525 he was appointed to a regular professorship in theology. We can be sure that he and his bride had at least one good meal in their first year of married life, for in his letter, Luther included thanks for the game which Spalatin had sent for the Bugenhagen's wedding celebration. Following the marriage of the Pomeranian, others of the monks began to forego their vows and marry. One of the first of these was Wenceslaus Link, successor to Staupitz as Vicar-General of the Augustinians in Germany, who was married by Bugenhagen in 1523.

Bugenhagen lived a very active life in Wittenberg. In addition to his duties as professor, he was preacher at the City Church where it was not unusual for him to preach every day in the week. He was a preacher of considerable power, drawing good crowds. Because he was frequently absent on his "missionary" journeys spreading Luther's doctrines throughout the German provinces, a substitute was often necessary. At such times, Luther was often called upon to preach in City Church, so much so that he complained to Link: "I am not only Luther, but Pomeranus, Registrar, Moses, Jethro, and what not—all things in all." He may have been "all things in all," but he was not Bugenhagen to the people, as we gather from the reports that these services were not always well-attended.

Preaching the Word was always of utmost importance to Luther, and he depended on his co-workers to do their share and to do it well. He appreciated the strong preaching of his pastor in the City Church which he attended when he was in town. In 1537, when Pomeranus was called to go to Denmark to consolidate the reforms there, the Elector gave him permission to leave Wittenberg, provided that his preaching and parish duties were adequately cared for. The plan was for the parish pastor to return before the year was out. Instead, he was gone for two full years. Martin was the "pulpit supply" in his absence, beginning a series on the Gospel of John in July 1537. When Bugenhagen returned, two years later, Luther was only on chapter four of the Gospel.

Bugenhagen evidently preferred Luther in extensis on St. John rather than Agricola in his pulpit. When he left for Denmark, he stipulated that Agricola was not to preach in his place while he was gone. Agricola had tried a new vocabulary to cover his leaning toward a softening of Luther's strong approach in his faith versus works position. Bugenhagen represented the conservative point of view of Luther, while Agricola was more Melanchthonian. When Bugenhagen was to be gone for an extended time, he wanted to be sure his people were exposed to the true Gospel, the complete adequacy of the grace of God. This was not rancor showing its face, but it was clear evidence of the divergence which emerged among Luther's colleagues after his death.

Bugenhagen's preaching led to other requests for his services. His preaching was a major factor in his first call to Wittenberg and gained him notoriety in the first years of the Reformation movement. Luther understood this, being himself a parishioner of the Pomeranian at the City Church. From time to time, Martin made suggestions to his colleagues and students about preaching. In one of his "conversations," he reminded his listeners that they should be humble in their preaching, realizing that the real good must come from God. Then he went on to illustrate, "Don't think about Melanchthon and Bugenhagen or me or any learned man, and try not to be learned in the pulpit."

This reference to the quality of Bugenhagen's preaching was tempered by Luther telling the preachers they should not be so long-winded, like chattering women, giving the back of his hand to Bugenhagen, who was, as he put it, "longuiloquent." On one occasion Luther told of a housewife who apologized for not cooking the Sunday dinner long enough. Her reason? She "thought Pomeranus was preaching today." Long-winded or not, reports indicate that Bugenhagen had a better congregation than any of his substitutes, including Luther.

When the City Council of Danzig asked Luther to come and establish reform in their city, he begged off, and refused also to send Bugenhagen, saying that he needed him for other reasons. "On your written request," he wrote, "I did my very best to get you a proper preacher. It was not possible to give you John Bugenhagen, whom you mentioned as the man you wished to have, for our church here was not willing to let him go, since we must keep men here by whom we can train other men and serve other cities too."

The attempt to begin the work of reform in Danzig came out of initial approaches in 1533. The people liked the evangelical doctrines and welcomed their being preached in the city. Before sending for help, the City Council itself began to introduce reforms, making evangelical worship mandatory in all the churches in 1525. It was after this start-up work had been done that Bugenhagen was requested. In refusing to send the Pomeranian, Luther insisted that he wanted to do the will of God, never knowing in which action the will of God might be manifested. When Bugenhagen did not go, Michael Hanlein was sent instead. As it turned out, King Sigismund of Poland compelled the residents of Danzig, in 1526, to return to the rites of the Roman Church, and there was no more evangelical preaching until 1543.

In 1522–1523, evangelical preaching was introduced in Denmark through the work of Herman Tost. He was soon joined by Hans Tausen, called the "Danish Luther" because of his strong preaching of Luther's teachings. Tausen had been at Wittenberg in 1524 and was appointed to Viborg in 1524. Under his leadership and aided and abetted by civil authorities who had been looking for the right time for such action, the Danish Church had by 1527 broken with Rome. By 1530, the monks were out of the monasteries and clerical marriage was common. At the request of the rulers, Luther drew up the "Church Ordinance," which became the basis for organizing churches and schools along Reformation lines. Christian II had visited Wittenberg in 1524. His son, Christian III, as a youth had attended the Diet of Worms, becoming devoted to the radical monk, Martin Luther. Through the sympathetic approach of the rulers, Carmelite monks strongly represented in Denmark pioneered in evangelicalism. Bugenhagen spent considerable time participating in reform activities in Scandinavia and was asked by Christian III to officiate at his coronation in 1537. Soon after the coronation, Bugenhagen ordained seven bishops, or superintendents, for the Danish Church. Following this, he assisted the monarch in a re-establishment of the University of Copenhagen on a Protestant basis. Among its primary programs was the training of clergy.

During this period, a Protestant reformation was also taking place in Finland and Sweden. What had begun in Schleswig and Holstein was carried into the Baltic countries, with Bugenhagen as a prime mover in both church and school life. A former pupil of Bugenhagen at Wittenberg, Michael Agricola, was the leading Reformer in Finland, setting up in the early 1520s a disputation with Catholic opponents. Later he led reforms in Riga, Reval, and Dorpat.

In addition to the time spent in "missionary" work in Scandinavia in the 1530s, Bugenhagen had been involved for some years with Reform work in England. A decade earlier, Robert Barnes had come to Wittenberg, seeking refuge as well as evangelical understanding. At Cambridge University he had headed a group that espoused Protestant evangelicalism. Having experienced persecution in England, Barnes found his way to Wittenberg where he came under Bugenhagen's influence. The Pomeranian had been in touch with other English-Church rebels and found in Barnes a willing pupil. The work of Barnes, influenced by Bugenhagen, was important in the burgeoning movement of dissent in England.

Bugenhagen through the years took a leading part in the reform of the Church and education in all of North Germany. From 1523 on, as towns and cities were caught up in the Reformation, they called upon Luther for help, and more often than not, he sent Bugenhagen to carry out reforms in worship, church organization, and schools. Patterned after reforms in Wittenberg, constitutions were devised, organizations were formed, and leadership was trained. This process continued to the death of Luther in 1546 and after. In 1529, after Luther had prepared catechetical posters, Bugenhagen made arrangements for their publication in Hamburg in Low German, providing for the general population to have ready access to the materials. When the people of Hildesheim drove out their bishop in 1544, Bugenhagen was called upon to introduce the Reformation there.

The support of pastors was a sticky question for the emerging Reformation churches with their financial support now coming from their constituencies. Many had to "moonlight" in other trades in order to eke out a living when they left the security of Church-supported livelihood. The congregations had to be educated to a totally new approach: to support clergy themselves. This was not a great problem for those who became pastors of urban churches. Preachers like Bugenhagen were comparatively well off, with good salaries and such amenities as libraries and assistants. Other Reformation leaders, such as Justus Jonas, Nicholas Amsdorf, and John Brenz, also served city parishes, in contrast to the country pastors who suffered real hardships. The workload, though, was pretty much the same for city and rural pastors.

While Luther was in the Wartburg "captivity," the University suffered from falling enrollment and lack of direction from leaders who were engaged in radical reform of the Church. After Luther's return, Bugenhagen assisted him in taking steps to reorganize and revive the University. This was important because of the place of education in the Reformation movement. Some have maintained, especially those who were opposed to the evangelical movement, that Luther's "Appeal to the Municipalities of Germany"—in which there was a strong emphasis for education to go hand in hand with reform—was an afterthought. However, the interest which he, along with

Bugenhagen, showed in the University was an indication that the treatise was no afterthought, but rather a true indication of the importance of education, fostered by the Reformation.

Much of the spread of the Reformation was through "Visitations," carried out by Melanchthon, Bugenhagen, and Amsdorf in Saxony, under the authority of the Elector and the overall direction of Martin Luther. The "Visitations" were a sort of modified inquisition into the affairs of parishes, both Catholic and Protestant, throughout Germany. The first visitation was in 1527, and they continued well into the 1530s. In connection with such visitations, Bugenhagen was called to organize Reformation churches in such cities as Hamburg, Lübeck, Pomerania, and Brunswick. The first visitation revealed a shocking state of disorder and the need for a much more thorough investigation. All members of each parish were examined, including priests, as well as worship services, schools and educational practices.

Conditions were so bad that the Elector demanded that something be done at once. He requested that Melanchthon draw up a "Church Ordinance" in order that there be a practical and constitutional reformation. The Ordinance was given to Luther and Bugenhagen for possible revision. According to Luther, the whole procedure was based on Apostolic tradition and practice, and was only placed in the Elector's hands because of expediency and the lack of evangelical authority. The Elector provided the authority, and Bugenhagen provided most of the zeal. The procedure was to go into a province or region and begin the examination, then the new ordinance was applied in every phase of community life, with special attention to the schools, including qualification of teachers, instructional materials and equipment, and adherence to doctrinal standards. The rapid growth of the Reformation, especially in Northern

Germany, was due in large part to the work of these visitors, such as Bugenhagen, and their emphasis upon reform in Church and school.

The development of the school system had important implications for the growing use of the German language in both theological and general publications. Besides keeping up with his work at the University and the City Church, Bugenhagen was constantly writing tracts and translations. In 1524, he published his "Interpretatio in Librum Psalmorum," a commentary on the Psalms. Even at this early date in Reformation development, there were differences in Zwingli's and Luther's views of the Lord's Supper. So, Bugenhagen resented it when Bucer translated his work into German, giving a Zwinglian interpretation of the Lord's Supper. Bucer had already fallen from grace by giving a sacramentarian slant to his translations of Luther's works.

In 1523, when Zwingli's "Commentary On True and False Religion" was published, Perckheimer and Bugenhagen wrote a reply giving Luther's viewpoint. The main contention here, as at Marburg later, was over the conception of the Lord's Supper. A little later new recruits took up the cause on both sides, with pamphlets from the pens of Bugenhagen, Melanchthon, Osiander, and Brenz, besides Luther, bombarding the poor students and peasants with his point of view, while Oecolampadius, Capito and Bucer kept the printers busy by publishing the views of the Swiss Reformers. Gerbel, in a letter to Bugenhagen, made an appropriate comment that out of the symbol of supreme love had arisen hate, wrath and enmity.

In 1527, Luther wrote to Spalatin from Wittenberg to report that a plague had struck in August of that year. "I am staying here, and it is necessary that I do so because of the terrible fear among the common people. And so John Bugenhagen and I are here alone with the deacons." And to John Brenz he wrote in November, "Bugenhagen sends you greetings. He is my only companion, since all the rest have fled because of the plague." Bugenhagen elected to remain with the Luthers, even though his wife was expecting the birth of their first child. Luther wrote in December to Jonas, "Deacon John intends to move out of your house and return to the parsonage. Pomeranus will await his wife's confinement at my place. May Christ gather us together again at one place. Amen."

In those days, childbirth was a very serious business. It is easy to see Luther trying to ease the mind of Bugenhagen, who must have alternatively thought of his parishioners who were trying to come to grips with death, and his wife who was about to enter the valley of the shadow from which so many mothers never returned. However, his wife lived and the parishioners recovered, and a Reformation was waiting.

There is little question that Bugenhagen was one of Luther's closest friends. He joined with the others who were physically close as neighbors in Wittenberg, participating in discussions on a variety of theological and Biblical themes. Bugenhagen knew his Hebrew; Luther was not a great Hebrew scholar. Together, Luther, Bugenhagen, Melanchthon, Cruciger, Aurogallus, Rörer, and others met each week in an informal Bible Club and worked together translating the Old Testament. They compared notes, made suggestions, explored meanings, and otherwise contributed. The final work, of course, was that of Luther, who wanted to be sure that this was to be a translation into the idiomatic language of the common man of Germany. He wanted to "make the prophets speak German."

When John the Constant, successor to his brother, Frederick the Wise, as Elector of Saxony, was faced with the threat of military action by the Emperor in 1529 he asked the four Wittenberg

theologians—Bugenhagen, Melanchthon, Jonas, and Luther—
to advise him. Several Protestant princes had proposed a
defensive union if the Emperor persisted in his effort to shut
down the Reformation "heresies." The theologians agreed that
this should be avoided for it would make the Gospel responsible for bloodshed and this would be intolerable. Besides, God
would take care of the Prince, and as Luther put it: "we must
keep our hands clean of blood and violence."

Bugenhagen, along with Melanchthon and others, was
actively involved in the discussions that led to the Augsburg
Confession. Prior to the Diet of Augsburg in 1530 where the
Confession was presented to the Emperor, the Protestant
princes asked, through Chancellor Brück of the Saxony court in
Torgau, for some statement of the principles on which they
could agree. Brück anticipated that the Emperor would ask for
such a written statement at the coming Diet. The first writing
went to Torgau in the hand of Melanchthon, but was primarily
concerned with "church usages and ceremonies," and had little
to do with the "articles of faith," which were thought to have
been covered in the earlier Schwabach Articles. At the Diet,
neither was considered to accurately represent the point of view
of the princes. The upshot was that Melanchthon then prepared
what we know as the Augsburg Confession. Ultimately it was
approved by Luther, Bugenhagen, and other evangelical theologians. In all the theological give and take, Bugenhagen was an
active insider, being recognized as one of the leading theologians among the Lutherans.

As an administrator and organizer, Bugenhagen also helped
Luther deal with a number of personal problems. As occasionally happens even in the best regulated churches, parishioners
sometimes were unhappy with their pastors. Such was the case
in Creuzberg, Thuringia, in January 1543. Their pastor, George

Spanlein, who had been an Augustinian monk, was quite offensive in his dealing with his people. Luther proposed transferring him to another parish, an action which had precedent in the solution of another such problem a week or so earlier. In each case he and Bugenhagen shared the decision and action.

There were disappointments in Bugenhagen's life, but probably none exceeded his disappointment at being left home when the theologians packed up and left for Marburg to dispute with the forces of Zwingli on the doctrine of the Lord's Supper. But Bugenhagen was the best man to keep the University going; in the words of Justus Jonas, "Bishop Bugenhagen was left at home to look after the University and take care of the Church." The only way he knew what was happening in Marburg was through the letters he and Katie Luther received from those who were in the thick of the discussion.

The meeting was set up as a conversation that might lead to some agreement on doctrines that were common to the various reform groups, but ultimately the sharpest point of discussion was on the matter of the Lord's Supper. Historians have written pages on what happened at Marburg. Luther told the whole story in a letter to Katie: "Tell Bugenhagen that Zwingli's best argument was that a body cannot exist without occupying space, and, therefore, Christ's body is not in the bread, and that Oecolampadius's best argument was that the sacrament is (only) the sign of Christ's body." Luther had gained his idea of the Mass from Staupitz, who in turn had studied under Biel. Luther could never agree with Zwingli that there was no real presence at the Eucharist. For Luther the bread was bread, and the bread was also the body of Christ.

Bugenhagen did not miss all the battles, however. The Anabaptists were stirring up much trouble for the Lutherans.

Melchior Hoffmann, a fanatical member of the Anabaptists, had been expelled from Kiel because he disputed with Bugenhagen over the Eucharist, and maintained the Zwinglian view. The Anabaptists had been established in Kiel with the official sanction of the King of Denmark, Frederick I, who later banished Hoffmann. Philip the Landgrave was also having his troubles with the sect and appealed to the Faculty of Theology at Wittenberg for suggestions as to procedure against the Anabaptists. The letter of advice which the faculty signed, drafted by Melanchthon and Bugenhagen, suggested that the leaders should be executed, and the lesser followers should receive severe punishment. The basis for such action was that the Anabaptists were guilty of civil disobedience and blasphemy.

The violence of the Lutheran opposition to the Anabaptists was reflected in the language used in disputes with them and all others who were in conflict with Luther's reformation leadership. These included the Anabaptists, Catholic Church leaders, those too radical in their reform practices, and leaders of other Reform Movements such as Zwingli, Oecolampadius, and Bucer. The in-fighting with the Anabaptists became bloody, the ferocity paralleled only by the verbal and written expressions loosed on opponents and the public.

Historians have called attention to the lewd, bawdy, barnyard, and often very profane language which was characteristic of the age. The Reformers, of all stripes and regardless of the pieties they proposed, were no exception in their language. The woodcuts and drawings of even major artists depict the "enemies" as vicious animals, in depraved and suggestive behavior. The greatest leaders—Luther, Erasmus, Bucer, Melanchthon—all joined in. And Bugenhagen also was one with them. In 1531, he spoke in such terms with John

Schlagenhaufen about his problems in theological under-standing. Schlagenhaufen was one of the Table Talk companions who collected and published Luther's comments, to the chagrin of Katie Luther, who thought income from sales of the published Table Talk should come to Martin, the "talker." Bugenhagen emulated Luther in language so coarse that even the Reformer took issue with his expression in such foul words. However, he suggested that such language was perhaps the only way to deal with the devil. And, Luther added, although there is little evidence that it was effective, "I often call my wife to help me ward off vain thoughts."

The social and religious turmoil of the decade between 1521 and 1531 caused a serious drop in attendance at all the German universities. While this was not as true at the University of Wittenberg, thanks to the Reformers who kept the University in the public eye, the leaders decided to try some means of getting new students. Before all of the trouble, giving University degrees only after a public disputation had given much prestige to the degrees granted. This practice had fallen off during the turmoil and now University officials thought they would revive it at Wittenberg to enhance their reputation. Among the first to receive the degree of Doctor of Theology after this reform were Bugenhagen, Cruciger, and Aepinus, the Hamburg Superin-tendent. Melanchthon drew up the theses for disputation, and the event took place in 1533; Luther presided. The disputants and members of the faculty were not the only celebrities present. Also there were the Elector and many other magnates; the envoy of Henry VIII; Barnes, soon to be martyred; and Alexander Alexius, a Scottish refugee, the last named taking part in the disputation. Bugenhagen was chosen to be the first to receive his degree in this manner, a matter of some privilege.

On some occasions Bugenhagen and others of the inner group co-signed with Luther letters on personal matters. In 1528, Luther wrote to Stephen Roth, in Zwickau, regarding problems between Roth and his wife, Ursula. She refused to go with Roth to Zwickau when he was appointed notary there. Roth suggested that she seek counsel with Luther in this disagreement. She refused, probably because Luther was the one appointing her husband. In a letter co-signed by Bugenhagen, Luther expressed the medieval concept of the husband as lord and master of the household. The letter began, "Grace and peace in Christ, and authority over your wife!" It went on to say that Roth himself should "not allow her to despise and trample underfoot the authority of the husband which is the glory of God, as St. Paul teaches." While Luther later moved gradually away from this rigid position, at least in his own relationship with Katie, his words were typical of the view prevalent in that day, and, typically, he found a rationale in Scripture.

Due to the so-called "treachery" of the Landgrave Philip of Hesse, Charles V was able to crush the Reform Movement in the territory of the Duke of Cleves. Then he promised a Diet of German representation, to which would be submitted a final settlement of the religious question. The Saxon Elector asked the Wittenberg theologians to prepare a statement of the concessions they would be willing to make to the Romanists. Melanchthon prepared a letter with the help of Bugenhagen, Luther, Cruciger, and Maier which in their concessions witness to the fact that there was some movement toward a more liberal approach by the Reformation leadership. The mark of Bugenhagen is plain throughout this particular struggle.

One would have thought that this city pastor had his hands pretty full, but Bugenhagen filled in his "spare time" with some noteworthy literary contributions, beyond those already mentioned. He was one of the group who met to revise Luther's translation of the Bible into German. Bugenhagen himself translated the Bible into Low German, thus making it available to even more of the public. He also wrote a history of Pomerania that remained unpublished until 1728 but was evidently a work of some merit, for it was published in a new edition as recently as 1901.

In and through all of these activities, Bugenhagen was always Luther's close friend. He performed the wedding ceremony for Luther and Katherine von Bora in 1525; he was with him during the plague; he executed in practical ways all of the ideas of Luther; and when Luther died, Bugenhagen delivered the chief funeral sermon. Luther had frequently been in poor health. Often Bugenhagen would rebuke him for beseeching God to take his life, and Luther would reply, "Only help me to my end with your prayers." With Justus Jonas, Bugenhagen made a study of the illnesses of Luther—each time thinking it would be his last—in order that men should possibly conquer the disease that was cutting down their leader and friend.

Apparently the friends of Luther, especially those close friends with whom he worked day after day, got along with each other even though they were distinctly different individuals. They were as close to each other as they were to their leader. Sometimes there was a little by-play among them, with pettiness occasionally showing. Luther tried to give a cup to Agricola, planning to send it with a letter referring to it as "that little vessel adorned with pewter." But he had to add a postscript, adding that Katie had not been a party to the giving; indeed she had conspired with Bugenhagen and Jonas, one of them evidently absconding with the cup.

This intimacy was illustrated at another time when Luther was quite sick with "the stone" while at Schmalkalden in 1537.

He called Bugenhagen to his bedside and dictated his will to him. That Luther should use the Pomeranian in this very personal matter was not surprising, since the Reformer once said that when he was depressed or blue "a word from Pomeranus or Philipp or Katie" would restore his spirits.

In his Table Talk, as recorded by Conrad Cordatus in 1531, Luther said that this was a rather common experience for him. "That those who are tempted may divert their thoughts, let them listen to the words of some good man, as to the voice of God from heaven. So I have often been refreshed by the words which Bugenhagen spoke to me: 'You ought not to despise my consolation because I am convinced that I speak words of God from Heaven.'" Such words were needed more often than we would perhaps expect, since Luther was up and down emotionally. His most aggressive leadership frequently came during and after these periods of self-doubt and fears for the success of the work he was doing.

Just how much Luther meant to his friends and associates is evident in the funeral sermon preached by Bugenhagen. Never had Luther feared anyone, said Bugenhagen. "Though to some he appeared too sharp and bitter in reproof and condemnation, this was his due prerogative as a prophet, as it was of Christ himself in his conflict with the scribes and pharisees. In his role as a prophet sent by God he rediscovered and vindicated the Gospel, and delivered the Church from the papal tyranny. . . . To Christian faith, death is but the beginning of eternal life. Dead in the body, Luther will live in his work in accordance with his own prophecy, which it is for his followers to fulfill."

Bugenhagen could not have described better his own life: he was one of the followers who was fulfilling the prophecy of Luther. Bugenhagen loved and served the Reformation to the end. He, more than any other, was responsible for the organization of the Reformation church in the German provinces. Pomeranus kept up his daily work in Wittenberg as a teacher and preacher until his own death twelve years after Luther's death, fulfilling the prophecy of the Reformer. Though Luther was no longer at his side, he was the brilliant mind and spirit that gave impetus to the Reformation. We see Luther through men like Bugenhagen.

CHAPTER 6

Justus Jonas

L uther had a reputation for being, as Bugenhagen noted in his funeral sermon, "too sharp and bitter in condemnation." Justus Jonas apparently matched him in character. An ex-lawyer, Jonas was apt to get angry over Luther's hesitation to agree with him, and Martin returned the compliment. Upon occasion, however, Luther seemed to back away from confrontation with his devoted friend. "I know," he told Jonas, "that I am ignorant of much. I have preached for twenty years and do not yet understand the passage, 'the just shall live by faith.'"

From the time that Jonas walked behind the cart which was bearing Luther to the Diet at Worms, to the moment when he leaned over to catch the Reformer's last words, the jurist turned theologian was a constant companion and adviser to Luther. Christened Jodocus (or Jobst) Koch, like many other Greek scholars of the time he changed his name to a Greek version, becoming Justus Jonas. He listened to the Leipzig Disputation between Luther and Eck in 1519 and was from that time a firm believer in the evangelical doctrines. Great movements frequently make great men, and the Reformation was a great enough movement to have made great the men who took part. Luther, though, seems to have surrounded himself with men who would have been famous without the movement. Although Jonas was only in his mid-twenties when he joined the Wittenbergers, one writer speaks of him as "Justus Jonas, the famous German Humanist."

As a youth he had come out of Nördlingen to study at Erfurt, where he received his baccalaureate in 1510. He stayed in Wittenberg for four years and was part of the University community when Luther began teaching there in 1512. While they were undoubtedly acquainted, there is nothing to suggest that the future Reformer made any great impression on him. In 1515 he returned to Erfurt to teach canon law. In 1519 he was named Rector of the University of Erfurt. As a humanist he revered Erasmus and with other scholars made pilgrimages to the Dutch man's home.

Erasmus agreed with Luther's criticisms of the Church, but he was convinced that the changes could be made from within. Erasmus was jealous for the life of the Roman Catholic Church and was disturbed by Luther's boisterous ways. A visit from Jonas, after the Augustinian became Rector at Erfurt, convinced Erasmus that something had to be done about Luther or a revolution would come.

While at Erfurt, Jonas went to Leipzig in 1519 and sat in on the Disputation between Luther and Eck, where he was impressed by the views of Luther—so impressed that he became a devoted follower. In 1521 when Luther passed through Erfurt on his way to Worms, Jonas began to walk behind the cart in which the Friar of Wittenberg rode, becoming in fact a Lutheran, for better or for worse. After the Diet of Worms, he returned with Luther to Wittenberg, there taking a position as professor of Canon Law under appointment of the Elector Frederick the Wise. He soon switched to the teaching of theology, that being the drawing card at Wittenberg. He wrote enthusiastically to a friend about the "unbelievable wealth of spiritual interests in the little town of Wittenberg."

From following behind the cart, Jonas soon moved to a lead position as a kind of advance agent for Luther, making arrangements for his stay in Worms. He was a good public relations agent. When the budding Reformer arrived at Worms, he was met two and a half miles from town by some two thousand enthusiastic people, led by Jonas. When Luther appeared before the Emperor, he had at least three loyal friends supporting him, even though the lack of a safe-conduct made them keep a low profile: Jerome Schurff, a lawyer from Wittenberg, Nicholas Amsdorf, and Justus Jonas.

While Jonas was becoming a leading figure in Luther's evangelical movement, he maintained contact with Erasmus. Erasmus held to his opinion that the followers of Luther were good men, even though he felt that the Reformer himself was too abrasive and that his writings were too controversial. To Spalatin he wrote in 1520 that Luther was "lacking in moderation," and that "Christ is not guiding his pen." Erasmus was quite concerned that such scholarly minds as those of Jonas and Melanchthon should be drawn into the disruptive and revolutionary ideas of Luther.

While there had been intimations that Erasmus might become a part of the Reform Movement, an open breach between the great humanist scholar and Luther, the impetuous prophet of the Reformation, became inevitable. In letters to Melanchthon, Jonas, and Leonard Prichard, between June 1519 and May 1521, Erasmus made it clear that he opposed a complete break with the past and that the Reform Movement was not for him. He was too faithful to the Catholic Church to be a party to the kind of excesses he was seeing and about which he was hearing. To Jonas he wrote of his confidence in Pope Leo X and Emperor Charles V, calling attention to their mildness as compared with Luther's lack of any spirit of the Gospel of love. To him, schism, conspiracy and factionalism were anathema. He was convinced, and so wrote to Jonas, that Luther was about to bring on a revolution, not a reformation.

Indicating his openness to a more receptive point of view, Erasmus wrote to Jonas about his support of Luther at Worms: "The report here is that you stood by Martin Luther at Worms. No doubt you did so, just as I should have done had I been there, that this tragedy might be so settled by moderate counsel that it would not afterwards break out again with greater injury to the world. And I wonder that this was not done, since the best men greatly desired that the tranquillity of the Church should be the matter of chief concern."

It will be remembered that when Luther was returning from the Diet of Worms, not trusting the safe-conduct guaranteed by the Emperor, he allowed himself to be "kidnapped" by the Elector Frederick's men. For fourteen months he was "Sir George," the knight, at the Wartburg. During Luther's absence from Wittenberg, Jonas took a leading part in the work of the Reformers, but without Luther's restraining hand, the situation there got out of control. Gabriel Zwilling, whose fiery preaching earned him the title "the second Luther," led the Augustinians and the townspeople in an iconoclastic revolt. They began to remove altars from the monastery chapel. Not satisfied with this, they joined a movement led by Carlstadt to remove the "emblems of idolatry" from all places of worship. Such violent

The Cathedral at Worms, site of the Diet of 1521.

actions were not favored by Jonas, Melanchthon, Amsdorf, and other cooler heads. Their lack of enthusiasm drew the rebukes of Zwilling, but the iconoclastic excesses were quite shocking to gentle men such as Melanchthon and Aurogallus, and to jurists such as Jonas.

It is possible that there was some less-than-good feeling between Carlstadt and Jonas, in addition to their disagreement about the nature of reform. Carlstadt had difficulty in getting along with most of the Reformers and other colleagues. He had been openly campaigning for the post of Provost of the Cathedral in Wittenberg, but that post was given by the Elector to Jonas, a relative newcomer in the community. Although Carlstadt was restored to the good graces of Luther and the others for a time, he later was in so much trouble that he was banished, forced to leave the Elector's territories.

In spite of the misgivings of many, Zwilling and Carlstadt, with the cooperation of the Augustinian monks, refused to conduct Masses, saying that they had become "works" which were now being substituted for "faith." The Elector strongly disapproved, since many of the Masses were endowed, bringing revenue to the Church. He appointed Jonas, Melanchthon, Amsdorf, Carlstadt, Platner, Dolsk, and Schurff to study the matter. They recommended that the Elector eliminate Masses, and establish the Lord's Supper, with both bread and wine to be given to the laity. The Elector then asked the committee to reconsider, which it did, only returning with added emphasis on the reforms.

The faculty agreed on the reforms, although they did not condone the violence. Jonas preached a powerful sermon in 1521 in which he called for doing away with Masses, vigils and indulgences. The sermon came on All Saints Day, and was preached in the Castle Church, with all the relics in the Elector's collection on display. Not content with just preaching, Jonas went from the pulpit and scattered the money-box funds, an action he would have condemned earlier when he and Melanchthon opposed the violence of Carlstadt and Zwilling.

Now the University group—Jonas, Melanchthon, and others—formulated an ordinance containing plans for an orderly change. Many concessions were made to the more violent Reformers. Among the subjects included were the Lord's Supper, the care of the poor, idolatry, prostitution, the abolishment of fraternities, and such, covering both religious and civil matters. The Elector, however, did not approve of the Ordinance, which had been drawn up late in January 1522, and demanded that the old Order be restored immediately, pending a general and authoritative decision on the question. The Bishop of Meissen, having already joined Staupitz in a condemnation of the excesses tied to Luther, was determined to carry out an imperial mandate condemning innovations, and applauded the Elector's approach.

Because of the furor, the Elector thought it would be prudent to oppose the Ordinance. In the face of the power of the Emperor, it is hard to blame the Elector for his attitude. Later he became a staunch defender of the new doctrines. But the effect on Jonas and Melanchthon was to dampen their enthusiasm for immediate reform. They were not made of the same stuff of leadership as Luther, who was then out of circulation masquerading as Knight George at the Wartburg.

Nor is it surprising that the University men were unable to cope with the situation. They were trying to do what was best in the face of the opposition of the Elector, in whose bounty rested their livelihood. On the other hand, they faced the scorn and ridicule of the townspeople who had been stirred into hasty action. Add to this the fact that Melanchthon was only twenty-four years old and Jonas about twenty-seven. Such youth should not have to decide the fate of continents; on February 20, 1522, they sent to the Wartburg and asked Luther to come home.

Luther was able to set things in order without much trouble. Curiously enough, in October of the year Luther returned from the Wartburg, Melanchthon and Jonas engaged in a dispute with Carlstadt, their recent opponent, and this time they upheld the radical view in the reform of the Mass. In the conflict with the more conservative followers in the matter of the Mass, Jonas was in the thick of the fight. He helped Luther develop a scheme of reform, and then he himself sent a letter to the Elector urging its adoption; but it was rejected. In addition to sending the letter and working on the plan for reform, Jonas was busy with activities of a public nature, showing his dissatisfaction with things as they were and his desire for change.

He had preached in December 1521 against indulgences and Masses for the dead, proving "by Holy Writ" that they were abuses. His scattering of the money-box funds was just one of a number of actions which were in contradiction to his earlier thinking, when he and Melanchthon were dead set against the violence of Carlstadt and Zwilling. When the canons of the churches sided with the Elector against Luther in the fight for reform of the Mass, some cast aspersions on the character of Jonas. Luther wrote to Spalatin about this: "Have not you and your prince treated Jonas with enough contempt, or are you going to stab this good man through and through?"

Being stabbed "through and through" is not unusual for Reformers, though they do not ordinarily expect it from their colleagues. This probably was not the only time Jonas was treated with contempt. Luther may have been heaping equally hot coals of fire on the head of Spalatin in a later exchange when the Elector's secretary, evidently weary of being caught between his friends and the interests and actions of the Elector, thought it best to retire. He asked Luther to support someone else for his position, and the Reformer replied that he could think of "no one better than Melanchthon, Bugenhagen, or Jonas." Fortunately for Luther and his cause, Spalatin kept the job.

Not to be outdone by others of the Wittenberg circle, Jonas married in 1522, the same year as Bugenhagen. The marrying of the monks did not take long, for in a few years not only Jonas, Bugenhagen and Carlstadt, but Luther and others followed Luther's advice to marry and save themselves from sinning.

In 1523 Jonas was one of the guests at the wedding of Wenceslaus Link, who had been Vicar-General of the Augustinians. It may be that seeing this marriage prompted Luther to designate a task to Jonas. The Vicar to the Bishop of Constance, Faber, had written a "ponderous effusion" attacking Luther and defending priestly celibacy. This was reprinted by Duke George of Saxony in 1523, before Luther had gone to the altar with Katherine von Bora. Luther proposed that there is no "vocation" of celibacy which the better Christians choose on the road to perfection, but God's call comes in everyday jobs. Jonas wrote, "This is the work which emptied the cloisters." He was given the task of answering Faber because, being recently married, he was more affected and better fitted to justify the blessings of priestly marriage than was Luther.

Jonas responded: "As for this tiresome compiler of quotations from the Fathers and the Councils, he had written nothing that (Luther) had not already refuted." With this contemptuous preface by Jonas, Faber, who had been eager to gain the honor of a reply from Luther himself, had to be content. And Jonas did not fail to remind him of his personal responsibility as episcopal

Vicar of Constance for the scandal of priestly concubinage in his own diocese. The reminder was certainly neither flattering to Faber's self-esteem nor gratifying to his keen desire to acquire notoriety at Luther's expense.

Luther himself was soon to know the joys of married life, and Jonas was one of the few invited to the simple ceremony, performed by Pastor Bugenhagen on June 13, 1525. Jonas expressed a more tender side of his nature in the letter he wrote to Spalatin, who was not able to be present: "Grace and peace from God. This letter will come to you . . . as the bearer of great news. Our Luther married Katherine von Bora. I was present and was a witness of the marriage yesterday. Seeing the sight I had to give way to my feelings and could not refrain from tears. Now that it has happened and is the will of God, I wish this good and true man and beloved father in the Lord much happiness. God is wonderful in his work and ways."

Jonas was one of those closest to Luther in all the disputations during the Reformer's life, sometimes becoming something of a cause for dispute himself. There was one contest, with the Antinomians, which was apparently patched up until Jonas led Luther off on a new "holy war." Agricola led a group which maintained that there was a fundamental antinomy between the Law and the Gospel and that the preachers should only preach the Gospel. Luther wrote to Jonas that the best thing they did at Torgau was "to bury the rumor of suspicion of disagreement."

In answer, Jonas wrote from Nordhausen, "The contention between Philipp and Agricola grieves me deeply, for I know that it could be distasteful to you and add to your already heavy trial, which we, your disciples, ought to lessen, not increase." One would have thought that Jonas's desire to relieve the burdens of Luther would have led him to steer clear of possibilities of more trouble, but this was not the case. In a few years, according to Agricola, "The machinations of Jonas . . . set Luther once more on the warpath."

Agricola appealed to the Elector who referred such cases to the faculty at Wittenberg. Naturally enough, Jonas, Bugenhagen, and others who supported whatever Luther espoused, recommended in this case that Agricola be apprehended as a dangerous incendiary. By the time they arrived at this decision, Agricola had felt the call to greener pastures and left town.

In 1529, Jonas was one of those accompanying Luther to the Marburg Colloquy with the Zwinglians. Although he did not take part in the actual disputation, this honor being reserved, or commanded, by the Margrave for Luther and Melanchthon, he did carry on conversations with Bucer in an effort to find some way to relieve the tension of the discussions.

We get from Jonas a good picture of the background and the participants in the colloquy. In a letter he writes to William Reifenstein: "On Friday after Michaelmas those who are the leaders of the opposing parties conferred privately, by order of the prince—Luther with Oecolampadius, Philipp with Zwingli. But they failed to come to an agreement, and the next day—the Saturday after Michaelmas—the colloquy was begun. . . . On the one side were Zwingli, Oecolampadius, and Hedio, and with them James Sturm, head of the Strassburg Council, whom you know, a man of no small ability; also Ulrich Funk, from the Zurich Council, and Rudolph Frey, a councilor of Basle.

"On the other side were Luther, Philipp, Eberhard von der Than, prefect of Eisenach, I, Jonas, Caspar Cruciger, and the rest of our party. Before the Prince, with all the councilors sitting around, was placed a table at which were these four—Luther, Philipp, Zwingli, and Oecolampadius. . . . Oecolampadius urged this argument for almost two whole days: 'Christ has a true body and is in heaven, but no true body can be in two places.' Luther would not permit Christ's words about the supper to be distorted, by force or by craft, from the clear words of Him who said, 'This is my body.'" Here Jonas suggests that there really is not any answer to this argument: "On the Sunday after Michaelmas the colloquy was resumed in hope of agreement, but when the dispute was prolonged until almost evening with our opponents holding to their error like grim death, and with us defending the side of truth no whit less zealously, it was given up, and I do not know whether there will ever be any agreement among us now about the sacrament."

His descriptions of the men taking part in the discussions are interesting because they are among the few contemporary records: "Zwingli is somewhat boorish and presumptuous; Oecolampadius is a man of wonderful gentleness of spirit and kindliness; Hedio is no less suave and broadminded; Bucer has the craftiness of a fox, making a perverse pretense of wisdom and keenness. They are all scholars, of that here is no doubt; the papists are no opponents at all compared to them; but Zwingli seems to have given himself to letters when the Muses were angry and Minerva unwilling." When Luther read the letter to his wife, Katie, she said immediately, "Hasn't the good man become venomous?"

One or two of the contentions in which Jonas took part were over a period of years. Luther argued with Jonas and the other jurists whether or not the Reformers or their patrons should be allowed, scripturally speaking, to defend themselves if attacked. In late October 1530, Melanchthon and Jonas, with Spalatin, tried to convince Luther that there could be justifiable resistance of authority. Jurists such as Jonas gave reasonable grounds for such resistance, and the theologians concluded that Scripture does not disagree, in the case of self-defense, including against the Emperor. The conclusion was that arming, then, is necessary for "any day other cases may arise where it would be essential to be ready to defend oneself, not only from worldly motives, but from duty and constraint of conscience." This kind of reasoning became the rationale for the soon-to-be-developed Smalkaldic League and changed Luther's mind on the matter.

Luther had written in 1530 to the Elector in reply to a request for counsel: "At your Grace's request I have inquired and taken counsel of my dear friends Dr. Jonas, John Bugenhagen, and Professor Melanchthon on the question whether it is allowable to defend oneself against the Imperial majesty in the event that his Majesty were to proceed against anyone, etc., etc. It is no wise proper . . . for the Gospel's sake." Within the next year Jonas, Melanchthon and Spalatin convinced Luther that armed resistance to forcible suppression of the Gospel was perfectly compatible with the Gospel.

Jonas, because of his juridical training and abilities, relieved Luther of much of the strain of administration. In a letter dated 1529, the Reformer shifted some of the details that had been making life burdensome for him: "Prepare yourself, make up your mind to it, my dear Jonas, that all who come to me seeking parishes, whether they are bellies or spirits, I will send them to you. This man I send is one of them. You will see what kind of a man he is. To me he seemed fitted for the field or plow; he might, indeed, make a sexton. You may find something else in him, for the spirit can deceive me and hide itself from me. Do as you please."

The Town Council of Erfurt gave rough treatment to some of the Lutheran pastors, giving rise in 1536 to discussions on the nature of the true church. Luther wanted to help his pastors, so when they were attacked in a sermon by Conrad Kling, a distinguished preacher and Franciscan Friar, Luther, Melanchthon, and Jonas sent a letter to pastors, urging them to hold their ground.

When Luther was arranging a special dinner for newly minted Doctors of Theology in 1535, with Bugenhagen and Carlstadt among the degree recipients, Jonas was called upon to make the preparations. "I hope, dear Jonas, you received my letter in which the sow instructs Minerva on what is to be said at the graduation exercise. The Grand Wizard our Lord Kate is sending you several pieces of silver with which you are to purchase birds with whatever else is edible . . . if you want to spend more, you will be reimbursed." The dinner was held at the Black Cloisters, with Kate providing the beer.

Jonas was one of those who revised the Articles of Visitation in 1532, as requested by the Elector John a few days before his death. The parishes had been rearranged; the incomes of the priests had been adjusted; ecclesiastical revenues had been appropriated for the schools, the ministry and the poor. But this revision had not worn much better than the others, and there was a reflection of the "greater excommunication" which Luther had strenuously denounced and opposed, but which Melanchthon, Jonas and others saw as the only remedy for the relaxed moral discipline becoming evident among the Mass of the people. Thus, while Luther was furnishing the moving ideas, Jonas and other leaders were interpreting and making them work.

There is a recurring note in the records of the meetings, disputations, documents and organizational pursuits as the Reformation progressed: The decisions made and recordings presented almost always bore the imprimatur not only of Luther, but of the close friends and colleagues surrounding him, in Wittenberg and beyond. The friends of Luther set their stamp of approval, sometimes with important modifications, on the Smalkald and Torgau Articles, the Augsburg Confessions, the Protest at Speyer, as well as approval before publication of some of Luther's most influential writings.

Jonas's family life was to a large extent bound up in the family life of the other Reformers. His children played with the children of Melanchthon, Luther, and Bugenhagen, and the parents gathered together in a rather exclusive circle for their social life. Perhaps this was to be expected, granted their closeness of interest in a common enterprise and the fact that they lived in close proximity.

The whole group seems to have enjoyed good food, Jonas proving himself a good host. When his friend, James Oethe from his native town Nordhausen, received his Doctor of Divinity degree at Wittenberg University, Jonas entertained him in great style with some game that Luther had begged from Spalatin and the Elector. Undoubtedly, some of the Wittenbergers raised their eyebrows at the goings-on in the Reformers' homes; they must have wondered whether these were compatible with the Ordinance which Jonas and others had helped draft while Luther was at the Wartburg. The Ordinance was one of the first attempts of civil authorities to introduce an evangelical form of worship; to mold social, political, and economic conditions; and to exercise strict supervision of public morality in conformity with the Gospel.

The children of the Reformers also were friends. Jonas, Melanchthon and Katie were the godparents for a son of Carlstadt, born in 1526, with Luther the baptizer. The first son of Jonas, Justus Junior, was a great friend and playmate of Luther's son, Hans, and Melanchthon's son, Philipp Junior. The little Melanchthon was "Lippus," and the little Jonas, "Jost," in their play. Once Luther promised them all an opportunity to play in a garden together—if they were good boys.

Jonas referred to his son as "the Dictator." When the family was at Nordhausen during the plague, Luther wrote, ". . . give your little Dictator many kisses for me and my little Hans. . . ." When Jonas wrote back to Luther, he showed like interest in the doings of the children: "I am glad to hear that your little son John is well and strong and active, and runs around and chatters, and is the joy of his parents. I am sending him as a New Year's present a silver piece, that he may have a little gift from Jonas and a token of the love I bear to him and his father . . . my son sends greetings to your daughter, his future wife."

The tender regard of each of the Reformers for the others who were engaged in the same enterprise was best illustrated at the time of the death of Melanchthon's son, George. Luther spoke of Jonas's capacity for tender feeling in a letter: "Last Sunday the Lord took from our Philipp his son George. You can imagine how hard we are trying to console this man whose heart is exceedingly tender and easily touched. It is wonderful how hard he takes the boy's death, for he has never before been tried with such grief. Pray for him all you can, that the Lord may comfort him, and write him a consoling letter with your well-known skill. You know how much depends on this man's life and health. We all grieve and are sad with him . . . of other things when our grief has somewhat abated."

The family of Jonas was ruled to a great extent by "the Dictator." The tendency to rule others persisted throughout his life, his arrogance being a source of trouble for his father. He was so arrogant that he used to despise his father, and say that he should have been born the son of a great king, and not of a theologian. He studied at Wittenberg, gaining his baccalaureate in 1539 and a master's degree in 1544. He studied law, instead of following his father as a theologian, and a few years out of University joined the service of the Duke of Mecklenburg. From this employ he went to that of the Elector August of Saxony, by whom he was suspected of disloyalty. In 1566 he was sent to Sweden to make a league between that country and Saxony against Denmark. During the journey he had the misfortune to be aboard a ship that was driven ashore in a storm into a Danish harbor. There he was captured and beheaded.

Jonas carried on much of the literary work that was common among the University faculties of the day. When Luther published a sermon against the Turks, Melanchthon and Jonas published a tract on the same subject, the actual writing being ascribed to Jonas. Luther wrote a number of hymns that still live, but only a few other poets are mentioned among the Reformers, one of them being Jonas.

Along with other classical scholars at the University, Jonas was one of those closely associated with Luther in his revision of the German Bible, being a member of the Bible Club—the Collegium Biblicum—which Luther called together regularly for help in translation. Luther's lack of background in Hebrew was given a boost by Jonas, Bugenhagen, and others.

Jonas, Luther and Spalatin all suffered from renal calculus, among other diseases. During one spell, Jonas took down all the details of Luther's reactions as part of a plan he and Bugenhagen had formed to determine the nature of the disease. The document is unique, for it purports to be a study of the disease, while, actually, it is almost entirely made up of the words Luther uttered when he thought he was going to die. The spiritual trial of Luther receives the greater part of the notation by Jonas.

The report begins with mention of one of Luther's periodic depressions. Then comes one of the only references to the actual physical pain: Luther "complained of a loud and troublesome roaring in the left ear, which the physicians said was the precursor of a fainting spell, and when he suddenly perceived that roaring the doctor said he could not sit because of it, and, going to his bed-chamber, lay down on the bed . . . he was seized with a faint. Suddenly he said, 'O Doctor Jonas, I am not well; give me some water or anything you have or I shall die.' Then, terrified and trembling, I poured cold water now on his face, now on his bare back."

This is the sole reference to Luther's physical condition except for his request that they remove his hose. It is probably just a coincidence, but Jonas then remarks "he suddenly felt all his strength leaving him." When Dr. Augustine came they applied hot bags and "fomentations," meanwhile encouraging him not to be downhearted. All the rest of the account, which is quite long, was devoted to noting the prayers and counsels of Luther, Bugenhagen, Katie, and Jonas.

If this is a good example of Jonas's and Bugenhagen's ability to note physical condition, it is no wonder that the disease of Luther defied them. Perhaps Jonas was more moved by the idea that he mentioned in a letter to Bugenhagen: "Because the sudden illness of our father Dr. Martin and other like occurrences seem to me to be warnings by which God admonishes us not to lay up for ourselves treasures of earth, as you exhorted us in today's sermon, I did not want the words that Dr. Martin used yesterday in his pain to be lost to us, for they are full of the most ardent feelings." This reported illness was in 1537.

In 1546 Jonas accompanied Luther, who hadn't been feeling well, to Mansfeld where Luther had been called to settle a dispute between the Mansfeld Counts. Besides Jonas, the three sons of Luther were in the party. Luther was not the only one who was feeling the effects of illness at this time, for in his last letter to Katie, he says, "I am not troubled with the stone, but Dr. Jonas's leg has become very bad, and has broken out on the shinbone." Jonas, though, was more interested in the Reformer's illness. He was in the room when Luther felt he had come to the end of his disputes. With others in the house gathered around, Jonas leaned over the dying man and asked, "Reverend Father, wilt thou stand by Christ and the doctrine thou hast preached?" Luther roused himself to say "Yes." It was his last word. With a deep sigh he passed away twenty minutes later.

In 1555 Jonas died at Eisfeld. He left his mark in a score of places, turning his back on a potentially great career as a Humanist. But he will be remembered longest as one of the intimate circle of friends who contributed so much to the life and work of Martin Luther.

Denying himself the possibility, even the certainty of success in one field of endeavor, he showed his true measure by turning to a new field under a comparatively untried leader, overcoming immense obstacles and attaining a greater success than most aspire to. Luther was without question the greatest of the Wittenberg theologians, but much of what he did depended on Jonas and the rest. A blunt man, outspoken, quarreling even with Luther when he thought there was reason, Jonas made friendship a treasured experience.

CHAPTER 7

Nicholas von Amsdorf

icholas von Amsdorf was one of Luther's early
friends. They spent time together in the halls of the
University. They shared views not only on the Bible
and theology, but on how to raise children, and on the intimacies of family life. Never married himself, Amsdorf nevertheless
was a part of Luther's home experiences. When Luther took a
few days off from his Wartburg "captivity," he slept at the home
of Amsdorf. Amsdorf was with Luther in Worms, and in other
of his celebrated experiences.

The close relationship Luther had with his Wittenberg
friends was one that did not depend upon their unanimity on
theological or biblical questions. To be sure, the basic point of
view of the Reformer was accepted by his friends and embraced
with enthusiasm. At the same time, they were independent
thinkers, and this was part of the mix that sustained their
friendship. There is no question that Luther modified his
approach to his central doctrine of justification by faith because

of his friends. As a matter of fact, later defenders of the faith considered this a black mark against some of them. On more than one occasion Luther declared that he should be the student, learning from Amsdorf and Jonas, and sitting under the preaching of his pastor, Bugenhagen.

Those outside the inner group recognized the closeness of these men to the Reformer, sometimes seeking through them to influence Luther. The leadership of the Roman Church saw this also and tried to use these friends to moderate the words and actions of the Reformer.

Interestingly enough, these close friends unanimously counseled Luther to be moderate in language and interpretation, but they disagreed among themselves on a number of important items. Some, who were part of the inner circle at one time or another, fell away, alienated from Luther because of these disagreements. Luther's closest friends, though, went along with him, in spite of their occasional misgivings. After his death in 1546, however, there was a schism between them which imperiled the whole Reformation Movement.

Nicholas von Amsdorf was born in Torgau, December 3, 1483, just three-and-a-half weeks after Martin Luther's birth. He became a scholar and a churchman, entering the University of Leipzig in 1500 and moving to the new University of Wittenberg in 1502. He earned his Master of Arts degree in 1504 and a Licentiate in Theology in 1511, becoming a professor at Wittenberg that same year. Luther had already begun teaching there in 1508, and the two became fast friends. While Luther seemed later to be drawn to younger colleagues, such as Philipp Melanchthon and John Agricola, referring to them sometimes as dearest friends, he referred to Amsdorf as a beloved associate.

Luther became the star of the Elector Frederick's University at Wittenberg, recognized as its leading theologian by

1515–1516. While such young intellectuals as Spalatin, Wenceslaus Link, and John Lang likely were drawn into Luther's circle because of his personality, Amsdorf came by way of his Augustinian studies. He too accepted the Augustinian theology and therefore was not surprised at the conclusions drawn by Luther, because he was on the same track.

When Amsdorf became professor of theology at Wittenberg in 1511, he and Luther became colleagues with a mutual admiration for each other. Evidently their closeness was recognized by others in the Reformation community. In 1519, seeking to calm Luther's increasing acerbity in his relations with the Pope, Otto Beckman wrote to Spalatin, urging that he "would do well to write to Amsdorf to admonish Martin not to speak so angrily without cause in public about the Pope and other prelates. We must go another road," he wrote. "The Church cannot be reformed by our contrivance, if it is to be reformed at all." However, Amsdorf was one of those who agreed with Martin in his strictures against the Pope. About this time, Christopher Scheurl was writing to John Eck, Luther's chief public enemy, concerning the theologians at Wittenberg who were giving trouble to the Church: "Among the most eminent are Martin Luther, the Augustinian, who expounds the epistles of the Tarsan with marvelous genius, Carlstadt, Amsdorf and others. . . ."

Luther agreed with such an estimate of the eminence of Amsdorf, writing to Spalatin in March 1518 about a problem in his preaching schedule: "I do not know whether I can preach on these three following days, but I will see; if not, my colleague, Amsdorf will supply my place." It is interesting that Luther signed this letter "Eleutherius. Br. Martin," using a Greek writing of his name that rarely appears in his writings or correspondence, perhaps suggesting his familiarity with Spalatin and Amsdorf.

When Luther requested of the Elector a change in courses of study at the University, he corresponded with Spalatin. In March 1519, Spalatin, representing the Elector, asked about who was involved in the request. Luther responded, "You desire to know who were the men who requested the Elector to change the course of studies. They were the rector, Carlstadt, Amsdorf, and I."

This was the year of the Leipzig Disputation, the celebrated debate between Luther and John Eck. Amsdorf accompanied Luther to Leipzig and played the part of friend and confidant of the Reformer, and he, unlike Melanchthon, took a public part in the disputation. That he was of some help to Luther is indicated by the fact that in August 1520, a year after Leipzig, Luther published the "Open Letter to the Christian Nobility of the German Nation Concerning the Reform of the Christian Estate," with a dedication to his "dear friend, the honorable and worthy Nicholas von Amsdorf, Licentiate in Holy Scriptures, and Canon in Wittenberg." There follows a letter of greeting which includes references to their common interest in the relation of the ruling classes to the life of the Church and asking Amsdorf to make any suggestions or criticisms about his writing. Undoubtedly Luther had confidence in Amsdorf's judgments, and understood his sympathies. Both the dedication and the letter reflect Luther's recognition of Amsdorf's influence.

Luther's friends went along to Leipzig because they had a growing sense of the significant theological, political, and societal directions in which he was moving; they were convinced by his sound reasoning and his strong persona. Amsdorf was so close to Luther and enthusiastic in his support that he encouraged the Reformer in statements and actions that were sometimes imprudent. Certainly some of the demands in the Letter to the Christian Nobility must have been shocking even to Luther's other friends.

Nevertheless, Martin felt close enough to Amsdorf to not only dedicate the writing to him, but to count on him for understanding and support. He was not mistaken in this.

Luther reflected on this in rather homey fashion a year or so later in comments on how things worked out: "I simply taught, preached, wrote God's Word; otherwise I did nothing. And then, while I slept, or drank Wittenberg beer with my Philipp and my Amsdorf, the Word so greatly weakened the papacy that never a prince or emperor inflicted such damage upon it."

However, Amsdorf did not always see eye to eye with Luther. In August 1520, Martin wrote to the Elector's secretary, recognizing that his own actions and those of his friends had caused some difficulty for the Elector. In his letter he specifically refers to Amsdorf's "excessive affection for the other side." There was no suggestion that Amsdorf should be punished, only that Luther was not pleased with things his friend had said and done. Upon occasion, other of Luther's closest friends suffered the displeasure of their leader; yet such outbursts did not disrupt their relationships.

We get some idea of Amsdorf's closeness to Luther from their experience at Worms and the "kidnapping" that followed. Nicholas was one of the little party that started off together for the Diet to which Martin had been summoned, and for which he had a safe-conduct from the Emperor. Traveling together were Luther; Jerome Schurff, a lawyer; John Petzensteiner, a young monk; a young Pomeranian humanist, Peter Suaven; and Father Nicholas von Amsdorf, of the University and the Cathedral. Justus Jonas walked beside the cart. They were all in some danger, for the Papal Bull Exsurge Domine, issued in 1520 after Luther's refusal to buckle under to Miltitz, specifically placed an interdiction on any who associated with the "heretic"—and they had no safe-conduct.

While Amsdorf was in seclusion in Worms, having been threatened with imprisonment by Aleander because of his lack of safe-conduct, Luther still had access to him for counsel and support, which he desperately needed as he faced the prospect of appearing before the Emperor and the highest dignitaries of the Church. He was basically shy, nervous and alone, expecting to be put to death. Before his appearance at the Diet, he met with Count Albert of Mansfeld to tell him of his meeting with the Archbishop of Trier. In his report to Albert, Luther recounted that the Archbishop had been quite gracious in his hospitality, extended also to Amsdorf and Schurff. When the Pope's representatives, Caracciolo and Aleander, reported to Rome, they said that Luther had refused to recant when approached by several of the princes. After the princes left, they said, the Archbishop of Trier invited Luther to his rooms, accompanied by Amsdorf and Schurff, "without whom he will take no step and speak no word."

Luther had not planned to have Amsdorf or other friends with him at Worms. He knew they were at risk in associating with him. He had written to several friends of a premonition that he was going to his death, but that he had no other course. Amsdorf was along because he was enthusiastic. He did not need to be asked to go to Worms; he wanted to, danger or no. When Luther left Worms, Amsdorf was with him, serving as a sounding-board for the Reformer's ideas and as a companion on his journeys.

Frederick the Elector provided the safe-conduct for Luther on the journey to and from Worms. Martin had stood up to a non-German Emperor and churchmen, which made a deep and lasting impression on the Elector, who was determined to see Luther's safe return to Wittenberg—this in defiance of the Edict of Worms. Aleander wrote the Edict, signed several weeks later by the Emperor, after Frederick the Wise and other German princes had gone home. The Edict affirmed the soon-to-be-published Bull of Excommunication and named Luther as a convicted heretic. His works were to be eradicated and his followers condemned to die with him.

With the Edict threatening, the Elector planned a kidnapping of Luther to take place at some point in the homeward journey from Worms. Some think that Frederick purposefully avoided knowing all the details of the plan so that he could protest his innocence of the plot. Probably Spalatin was privy to the details, perhaps actually being the one who saw that they were carried out. While Luther was not told everything that was going to happen, he wrote to his good friend, the painter Cranach, "I am going to allow myself to be imprisoned and hidden, though I don't know yet where it will be." With Jonas, Schurff, Petzensteiner and Amsdorf he set out for Wittenberg. At Eisenach, where he had once been a schoolboy, the party split. Jonas, Schurff and a student went on to Erfurt and Wittenberg; Luther, Amsdorf and Petzensteiner turned southeast to visit Luther's relatives in Mohra.

As they rode slowly in their cart from Mohra, some miles along the way they were accosted by many armed men who dragged Luther to the ground. Amsdorf, possibly in on the plot, loudly protested their actions but was able to escape along with Petzensteiner. They carried news of the attack to Wittenberg, where general mourning ensued. By this time Martin was safely settled in the Wartburg, a castle outside Eisenach to which the captors had circled back, one of several castle-garrisons controlled by the Saxon Elector. It is not known whether Amsdorf knew exactly where Luther had been carried, but he gave an exciting account of the kidnapping to the citizens of Wittenberg.

With Luther out of the picture, Carlstadt and Zwilling, two of the more radical Reformers, led in carrying out a variety of reforms in church practices at Wittenberg and at the University: communion was served in both kinds, bread and cup; priests and nuns were married, sometimes to each other, Carlstadt being one of the first to take this step; images were taken from churches and destroyed.

Hearing about this, Luther admonished Amsdorf and Melanchthon for going along with the Carlstadt-Zwilling reforms, and in December 1521, he slipped away from the Wartburg and spent a couple of days in Wittenberg in order to have a personal look at what was happening. He went to the home of Amsdorf, meeting there with Melanchthon and others of his close friends. Present were Luther, Melanchthon, Jonas, Bugenhagen, and Amsdorf, the host. Lucas Cranach, being sworn to secrecy, was called in to make some drawings of "Junker George" while the Reformation leadership talked. Amsdorf's lodgings were looked upon as a safe haven for these friends, all of whom risked their lives if discovered by the authorities. Being with Luther put them all under the Edict of Worms. After a close look at the situation, Martin was convinced that Philipp and Nicholas were on top of things and that Carlstadt was just his enthusiastic self, and so he returned to the Wartburg.

In the next couple of months, however, there were reports of more and more violence and more excesses. In March 1522, Luther decided to leave the Wartburg, without letting the Elector know, and returned to Wittenberg with his confidence in Amsdorf and Melanchthon's leadership somewhat shaken.

Upon leaving, Luther spent a day and a half with Amsdorf, Schurff, and Melanchthon, discussing the excesses of Carlstadt and Zwilling and what should or could be done to check them.

In the Reformer's view, focused by his studies and writing in the Wartburg, God was really in charge, and God alone would see to necessary changes in the Church and its practices. He believed this was Scriptural and therefore authoritative. Hence, he concluded that the Prince, as instrument of the Lord, should not use violent force, but depend upon God's will to prevail. Luther then wrote to Spalatin, urging him to keep the Elector from persecuting the fanatics. The Elector had difficulty in such restraint, since he believed in the Church, revered the saints, had great collections of relics, and thought, as did most of the ordinary citizens, that the destruction of images and the marriage of priests were alike blasphemous.

Amsdorf also was a close personal friend of the Reformer and his family, not only in matters of theological import, but in other matters as well—although just about every encounter was couched in biblical-theological terms. It was a two-way relationship. Although Luther was the acknowledged leader he was willing to learn from his friend. Luther on numerous occasions expressed a desire to be a student at the feet of Amsdorf or Bugenhagen or Melanchthon. From the Wartburg, he wrote Amsdorf: "I would like to be your student in the course in Hebrews and Psalms, in the course on Colossians . . . It is not you who need me, but I who need you. . . ."

In 1523, when Luther was gaining a reputation as a theologian and scholar, on one hand, and as a rabble-rouser on the other, even young ladies-in-waiting to the wife of Duke George of Albertine Saxony were found to be reading the monk's writings. Duke George was a strong Catholic Prince, at considerable odds with his cousin, the Elector Frederick, and well on his way to becoming an implacable foe of the Reformer. The three young women were dismissed by the Duke and left to shift for themselves. Amsdorf became aware of the situation. He thought that since they were guilty only of having read Luther's writings, that Luther himself should offer them some words of consolation. At his request, Luther wrote to the three young ladies, noting that while he did not know them, he perhaps shared responsibility for their predicament. His letter seems a little strange to modern minds, but his friend had asked him to write and he did.

Luther sought help from Amsdorf and other of his colleagues for help in finding mates for the twelve nuns deposited on his doorstep the day before Easter in 1523. The laymen who had rescued them from convent life thought that the Wittenberg Friar would care for them, since he was the leading exponent of their desire to live a normal family life. Martin himself was a celibate monk at the time and had to endure some crude remarks about being host to the renegade nuns. Amsdorf too became a matchmaker, putting out the word that the nuns were ladylike and pleasant to the eye, with good family backgrounds, and all under fifty. One was the sister of Luther's old master, Staupitz, who also happened to be Amsdorf's uncle.

They asked Spalatin to do what he could to get food and clothing from the Elector's court, since the ex-nuns were without funds and found their families slow to respond to their needs. Six of the nuns were finally cared for by their extended families; all of the six eventually finding husbands. Two of them, sisters, became live-in household help for the Lucas Cranach family. This left only Katherine von Bora, who took a place in the household of a lawyer named Reichenbach. While in his service, she met and fell in love with a former student of Melanchthon, but his parents resisted the idea of his marrying a former nun.

Amsdorf kept trying to find a husband for Katherine; his favorite prospect was the pastor at Orlamunde, Kaspar Glatz.

She was not impressed, however, and preferred to keep on working. When Amsdorf persisted in pushing Glatz, extolling his virtues, she responded that she would marry no one except Amsdorf himself or Luther. When Amsdorf told Luther what Katie had said, he scoffed at the idea, but it eventually found a responsive chord, and to the surprise of all their friends, Martin and Katherine were married in June 1525. Although Amsdorf was successful bringing about marriages for all the nuns, he himself did not marry.

A few months after the marriage of the Luthers, Spalatin also married. Even though he received a special invitation to attend, and good friend that he was, Luther did not attend the wedding. He sent his regrets explaining that Katie, his new wife, had a great respect for Amsdorf's opinions, and Amsdorf thought Luther was in danger from those "raging" against him. Luther's respect for the judgment of Amsdorf remained undiminished.

In 1524, Amsdorf went to Magdeburg to develop Church reforms there, becoming one of a group of outstanding preachers and theologians who, under the leadership of Luther, were remaking the Church in Germany: John Lang, a classmate and friend from student days was at Erfurt, now as a pastor rather than an Augustinian monk; John Brenz became a Reform leader in Swabia, preparing a catechism for use in Schwabisch Hall before Luther himself wrote of such material. The theology of Brenz was important in the much later development (1563) of the Thirty-nine Articles of the Anglican Church.

In the years that followed, Amsdorf continued as friend and confidant of Luther, although at a distance. His work as Reformer at Magdeburg was so effective that when he died in 1565, Magdeburg had replaced Wittenberg as the center of the Lutheran Reformation. Even after he had left Wittenberg, he carried on a vigorous correspondence with Luther and others in various councils and disputes. Many of the letters dealt with family and friends, personal matters that create bonds of friendship and concern. Other correspondence addressed matters relating to the Reformation and Luther's involvement in situations which grew out of his aggressive approach to things economic, political, and civil as well as religious.

Luther leaned on Amsdorf whenever melancholy set in or when problems needed more thought for solution. From the time Amsdorf took the assignment to Magdeburg until the death of Luther, the two were separated geographically, with the Reformer maintaining leadership of the movement from Wittenberg. Through mutual friends and correspondence, however, they stayed close. In 1529 Luther wrote to Amsdorf in the tenderest of language, asking him to be godfather to his little Magdelena. Magdelena was named for a beloved aunt who had lived with the Luthers in the Black Cloisters. After noting that God had given him and Katherine a daughter, he urgently asked Amsdorf to be her "father in God" at her baptism, to "bring this little heathen into the Christian fold."

When Luther was at the Marburg Colloquy with the Swiss Reformers in 1529, Amsdorf was not able to be among the participants, but Luther gave him a blow-by-blow account by regular messenger. Amsdorf stayed close to Luther in the free-will controversy with Erasmus, a position he reiterated during the development of the Smalkald Articles. In 1536, the Elector John Frederick was one of those summoned to Mantua in Italy for an imperial council with Church leaders. He asked Luther to prepare materials to take with him in his capacity as a Protestant prince. Luther in turn, after writing out some suggestions for the prince, asked Amsdorf and others of his friends to look over what he had written. Mantua refused to host the meeting and John Frederick, therefore, did not represent the

German Protestant princes. The material prepared by Luther and edited by Amsdorf and others subsequently became the basis for the Smalkald Articles which were later approved by a convention of Protestant leaders. Eventually they were incorporated into the Articles of Faith of the Lutheran Church.

While Amsdorf kept in touch with Luther on all the ins and outs of the negotiation and setting out of positions, he was the busy pastor in Magdeburg, establishing Reformation churches and assisting in organizational work in nearby communities. He also kept in regular touch with Jonas, Bugenhagen, and other leaders who were advancing the Reformation in Pomerania, Halle, and Wittenberg. These men, though overshadowed by Luther, should also be recognized and remembered for the important part they played in the Reformation.

In 1541, the Bishop of Naumburg died. The normal process on naming a successor was for the clergy chapter to meet and choose the person to be named bishop by the Prince. They met and chose Julius von Pflug, a man of ability and integrity and a loyal Catholic. Duke John Frederick, however, insisted upon a Protestant, an evangelical, and named Nicholas von Amsdorf bishop, noting that he was of noble family, unmarried, and competent.

The power of the Elector was so great that he prevailed, and Amsdorf left Magdeburg to establish the Reform services in Naumburg. The appointment was controversial and marked a point of no return in negotiations which had been going on to repair the breach in the Church. This breach worsened when Luther was asked to participate in the consecration service, suggesting that his action was a return to a "purer" apostolic succession. This concept was in keeping with Luther's earlier pronouncement that the Pope could not excommunicate him— he would excommunicate the Pope.

Protestant Evangelicals were made bishops at about the same time in other important sees. In addition, the Church had to deal with the defection of the Elector and Archbishop of Cologne, Count Herman von Weid. While not nominally separating from the Catholic Church, Weid asked for and got help from Martin Bucer and Philipp Melanchthon when he accepted Luther's views and reformed worship life in his diocese.

All the while these explosive changes were taking place in Cologne, Halle, Regensberg and other cities, Pflug was trying to hang on to the see of Naumburg, a position he thought was rightfully his since he had been duly elected by the clergy. Amsdorf, however, had the continuing support of the Elector and regularly received support from Luther, to whom he frequently wrote for advice and to describe the discouraging nature of the work. The Reformer wrote to Amsdorf on July 14, 1543, explaining why he had not made a planned visit and reassuring Amsdorf that he was doing the work of the Lord. "According to his will, we must live, be cheerful, and endure whatever may befall. Even if what we endure and suffer please no one else, it is enough that is it well-pleasing to him."

Nicholas was not only having problems carrying out reforms in Naumburg, he also was having problems of theological interpretation with other Protestant leaders. It was not a time of smooth sailing as the German leaders dealt not only with the Catholics, but also with other Reform Movements, such as the Anabaptists, the Swiss, and the humanist thinkers within their own ranks.

Luther was very plain-spoken. In their continued search for avenues of rapprochement with the Church, Amsdorf and others occasionally raised questions about Luther's language and name-calling and were put off by his insistence that such expression was only a realistic appraisal of the great evils of the

Church and its leaders. Their misgivings about Luther did not lead to any break with him but probably made it easier for division to come among his followers after his death.

Amsdorf and Melanchthon were colleagues of Luther on the faculty at Wittenberg and were among his early and continuing supporters. This did not mean they were always in agreement, however. In the dialogue between Luther and Erasmus on free will, Melanchthon, with his humanist background, leaned toward the Dutch scholar, while Amsdorf was more Lutheran, more Augustinian. Melanchthon gave expression to a softening of the position of Luther on the doctrine of good works, but Amsdorf remained quite orthodox in his support of Luther's more rigid views.

When Wittenberg moved away from orthodox Lutheranism after the death of Luther, Amsdorf was one of those instrumental in founding the University of Jena, one of the first "Protestant" universities, and the new seat of orthodoxy for Luther's followers. Especially after Luther's death, Melanchthon served as a balance-wheel between the extreme expressions of Flacius of Jena, and the conservative expressions of Amsdorf. There needed to be a balance-wheel, because without the driving personality of Luther, around which his friends revolved, they went off in various directions and frequently were in conflict with one another. These differences of opinion led to a complete breach after Luther's death between some of those who had been most intimately associated with him. In the successive development of the Schwabach Articles, the Smalkald Articles, the Smalkald League, and finally the Smalkald War, 1546–1547, lines were drawn which finally resulted in an open break between Melanchthon and Amsdorf in their later careers. The two had been at odds on a number of issues, but their relationship with Luther kept them from a public display of their differences.

In 1544, Melanchthon wrote a little book on the Eucharist called *Herman's Consultation*, after Archbishop Herman of Cologne. The book was received with favor by the clergy, but the Elector felt that Melanchthon was leaning toward a spiritual interpretation of the Lord's Supper. He asked Amsdorf for his criticisms, and Nicholas sent a copy to Luther. He also sent his unfavorable reaction to the book, which caused Luther to break with Melanchthon for a time. Luther wrote his own response to the book but did not break completely with Bucer or Melanchthon, even though both expected him to do so. The Elector's chancellor, Gregory Brück, noted that "Philipp and Martin are still quite good friends."

Amsdorf had several years before insisted to Luther that Philipp was guilty of sacramentarianism, but had been unable to convince the Reformer. Luther, therefore, did not abandon Philipp, in spite of Amsdorf's criticisms, saying the he had no suspicions with regard to Melanchthon. The whole dispute indicates that while Amsdorf and Melanchthon may have been on opposite sides of some very important issues, their relationship with Luther was strong enough to withstand some heavy conflict. The two friends of Martin remained such, although they gradually distanced themselves from one another.

On June 3, 1545, Luther wrote to Amsdorf, then at Naumburg, as they contemplated diets and councils, saying that he wasn't concerned about them and that he expected nothing to come from them. A month later he wrote again noting that they were both getting old, calling attention to the difference in authority and position of the Pope and the Emperor, and saying that he was worn out and sick from all the problems involved in the Reformation enterprise. "My torture, the stone, would have killed me on St. John's Day (June 24) had God not decided differently." Such references were common in his correspondence with Amsdorf and other friends, especially in his later years. They were more than colleagues in theological and philosophical battle—they were friends.

After the death of Luther in 1546, there was division among his followers, deriving mainly from the earlier sacramentarian controversies. Melanchthon and Bucer led a group, sometimes called the "Philippists," holding to a position closer to that of the Zwinglians. Their emphasis was on the concept of the elements as something of a memorial proposition, with spiritual rather than corporeal character. Amsdorf was the leader of the conservative back-to-Luther group, holding almost to the traditional Catholic view that when the priest raised the host the elements became the veritable body and blood of Christ. While they objected to the concept of the "miracle of the Mass," and refused the idea that transubstantiation took place through the elevating gesture of the priest, their view followed that of Luther, expressed most vividly at Marburg: *Hoc est corpus meum*—this is my body.

At about this same time, George Major and Melanchthon were responsible for drawing up what became known as the Leipzig Interim. The leading conservative Lutherans refused to accept this, saying it was not an acceptable expression of the Reformer's positions, and it would lead the ordinary person to believe that Catholic doctrine would be revived. The Leipzig Interim was one outcome of the Augsburg Interim of 1548, both of them being attempts to establish some kind of harmony between political and theological concepts. The objections to the Augsburg Interim by both Catholics and Protestants led to Melanchthon writing the Leipzig document in an effort to save the Evangelical position, with particular emphasis upon the basic Lutheran doctrine of justification by faith.

Melanchthon, though, did not convince Mathias Flacius, Amsdorf, and others in Magdeburg and Jena. Flacius, professor of Hebrew at Wittenberg, and Amsdorf strongly suggested that Melanchthon had compromised Luther's teachings in the Augsburg Interim and in the Leipzig document. The upshot of this controversy was a division of the followers of Luther into two camps, one led by Melanchthon and the Wittenberg professors, the other led by Amsdorf and including Flacius, Gallus, Stolz, and others from the Jena faculty.

In 1547, the armies of the Smalkald League were defeated by the forces of Charles V, and the Elector John Frederick was taken prisoner and forced into exile, giving up his electoral credentials to a relative, Duke Maurice. This worthy had betrayed the Protestants, selling out to the Emperor in the interest of future preferment. Amsdorf, Lucas Cranach, Justus Jonas, and others who considered themselves faithful to Martin Luther, followed their prince into exile. Amsdorf was deposed as Bishop of Naumburg, and Julius von Pflug was finally in the position for which he had contested.

In his last year, Amsdorf lived in Eisenach, embroiled in many quarrels and serving as the leader of the group which thought of itself the "genuine Lutherans." The Philippists, led by Philipp Melanchthon, were denounced as temporarians, those who, while holding firmly to basic Lutheran doctrine were willing to temporize in such matters which in their judgment were non-essentials. Magdeburg, where Amsdorf spent many years, became the great stronghold of "genuine Lutherans" in Northern Germany. The University of Jena, which Amsdorf helped found, replaced Wittenberg as the center of Lutheran influence.

While Nicholas von Amsdorf is comparatively unknown, even to many Lutherans, the great Reformer looked upon him not only as a close friend, but as someone of real importance to their common cause. He was asked by Luther to assist in translating the Bible, including checking Luther's own work. When Luther found it necessary to be gone from Wittenberg, Amsdorf took his place in preaching and teaching. Luther called Amsdorf a natural-born theologian. In Amsdorf's last years he was proclaimed the "Secret Bishop" of the Lutheran Church in Eisenach. Today his work is acclaimed by some scholars as more important to the German Reformation and the Lutheran Church than the work of such stalwarts as Melanchthon and Bugenhagen. He kept the faith.

CHAPTER 8

George Spalatin

In August 1516, Luther wrote to the Elector Frederick's secretary and librarian: "To my friend Georg Spalatin, servant of God, Jesus. Greetings. I seek a service, Dearest Spalatin . . . please loan me a copy of St. Jerome's letters for an hour, or at least (I would like this even better) copy for me as quickly as you can what the saint has written about St. Bartholemew the Apostle in the little book *On Famous People*. I need it before noon, as I shall be preaching to the people." So Martin Luther, as he did on many, many occasions, called upon one of his close friends in a moment of immediate need. In this case the need was not great, but in others the need was related to the important business of carrying on the Reformation. Spalatin responded here as always with the kind of help and support that contributed so much to Luther's effectiveness.

It is estimated that Luther wrote over 800 letters to Spalatin, yet he is one of the least known of German Reformation leaders. Born Georg Burckhardt, in Spalt—a village some thirty miles south of Nuremberg, from which he took his name—on January 17, 1484, he was sent to Erfurt for schooling. There he was a classmate of Martin Luther. There is little to suggest that they were acquainted more than casually. Spalatin received his baccalaureate in 1499 and went with his favorite professor, Nicholas Marschalk, to Wittenberg in 1502. There he received his master's degree before returning to Erfurt in 1505 to study jurisprudence. He maintained friendly relationships with the humanists Erasmus, Reuchlin, and others. For several years he was a monk in St. George's monastery in Erfurt and was ordained into the priesthood.

In 1509, he was asked to tutor the son of the Elector Frederick who resided in Torgau, about twenty miles from Wittenberg on the Elbe River. In 1512, the year that Luther received his doctorate, Spalatin was named librarian and counselor to the Elector, a position which later on gave him many opportunities to be helpful to Luther. Wittenberg was close enough that he visited frequently, being on friendly terms with the faculty there, especially with Luther.

Luther and Spalatin corresponded frequently, so frequently in fact that one wonders how they had time for the many activities that concerned them. In the trivial matters as well as matters of state, in personal and family interests, in major concerns of the University as well as the financial well-being of his colleagues, whatever concerned Luther seemed to be of interest and concern to Spalatin, and they exchanged letters in every regard.

It would be difficult, if not impossible at this distance in time and place, to say who was "best friend" of Martin Luther throughout his career. Arguably it could have been Justus Jonas, John Bugenhagen, Philipp Melanchthon, Nicholas von Amsdorf, or perhaps Lucas Cranach. There is no question, though, that none was a better friend than George Spalatin. For a man with so many personal quirks, Luther was fortunate to find so many who could see him and see beyond him and become and remain such good, supportive friends through the decades of his leadership of the German Reformation. Spalatin was one of these—perhaps first among equals.

Spalatin and Luther became collaborators in the work of reform about 1512. Spalatin, who was working for the Elector as liaison with the University, found Luther to be, in his opinion, the most important man in the University. He thus consulted with him before all others regarding the Elector's concerns. Luther apparently had charismatic appeal for Spalatin. But Spalatin also recognized Luther's quality of character and his competency as a scholar. Apparently the respect and admiration was mutual; their friendly, collegial relationship lasted thirty years. Spalatin's letters to Luther are largely lost, but Luther's responses remain and give us insight into the strong bond between the two men.

Spalatin was the trusted adviser to Frederick the Wise, Prince of Saxony and Imperial Elector. He won the support of the Elector for Luther and the Reformation movement, although to his death the Elector maintained his faithfulness to his Roman Catholic heritage. It was only on his deathbed that Frederick indicated any personal acceptance of Reformation doctrine and received communion in both bread and wine. The first of the Electors to receive a completely Lutheran education was John Frederick, nephew of Frederick the Wise, at the hand of Spalatin. John Frederick later became Elector, in 1532.

In his own right, Spalatin too was a writer and a theologian. Luther called upon him to help in the translation of the Bible, looking on him as his superior in proper interpretation of many words and phrases in Scripture. Spalatin did not engage in the polemical writing style of Luther. He translated the Latin writings of Melanchthon, Erasmus, and Luther and wrote biographies of the Electors Frederick III, John the Constant, and John Frederick.

After the death of the Elector Frederick in 1525, his brother, John the Constant, succeeded him as Elector. He also frequently turned to Spalatin for guidance. Spalatin at this time was serving as canon at Altenburg, a post to which he had accepted appointment at the time of the death of Frederick, and which he held until his own death in 1545. From Altenburg he continued to influence the Elector John, and his son and successor, John Frederick. With them and through them, Spalatin had a considerable hand in the emerging Reformation establishment. While Luther and Spalatin each married a Katherine in the same year, Martin did not attend his friend's wedding because his Katie was afraid of the possibility of violence along the route to the wedding. Spalatin was at Luther's wedding celebration, however, on June 27, his invitation from Luther being quite insistent: "You must come to my wedding," with an added word on the kind of thinking all the Reformers must have been doing in a time when nuns marrying priests and monks was the greatest of revolutions in religious and social behavior: "I have made the angels laugh and the devils weep." With Melanchthon having married Katherine Krapp, Luther's marriage to Katherine von Bora, and Spalatin's to Katherine Heydenreich, there must have been some confusing situations when the families were together, as they frequently were.

Spalatin maintained a residence at Torgau, the seat of the Elector Frederick. Because of his early acceptance of the Reformation principles and leadership, Torgau became a center of reform in religious and civil practice. His close colleague in Torgau was Gabriel Zwilling, called by some the "second

Luther" due to his fiery preaching and support of Luther. The accolade came despite Luther's displeasure for Zwilling's participation with Carlstadt in the objectionable reforms in Wittenberg while Luther was in "captivity" at the Wartburg.

Because of his position at the court of Frederick, Spalatin was well-situated to advance the Elector's support and defense of Luther. There is no clear record of meetings between Luther and Frederick, only that they were in the same room on several occasions with many others present. But there were many, many contacts through Spalatin. Luther's access to the Elector through Spalatin continued even after Frederick's death, with both his brother and his nephew who succeeded him. Spalatin was held in esteem and some veneration by them until he died. A modern archivist in the village of Spalt notes that "The most famous citizen of our town was Spalatin, a monk who helped Martin Luther introduce the so-called Reformation," as well as calling attention to his eminence as counselor to the Elector.

The successive Electors were among the most important princes of the Empire, which made Spalatin very important to the growing Reformation movement. His influence served to protect Luther on numerous occasions and made certain of the personal concern of the Elector, along with the Elector's support of Luther's theology and leadership. Actually, the Elector upon occasion expressed doubt and apprehension about Luther but was constrained to protect and support him on the advice and assurances of Spalatin, who had his complete confidence. The Electors John the Constant and John Frederick were from their youth and young manhood good followers of Luther, aiding and abetting the Reformation in keeping with the training and advice they had from Spalatin.

Many authorities are convinced that Luther would have lost his life and the Reformation would have failed if not for

Spalatin's influence with the Elector, especially in the early and crucial years, 1517–1521. The support which Spalatin urged was given, in spite of the reservations of the Elector in regard to Luther's theology and Luther's actions. In their early acquaintance, Spalatin was somewhat alone in his support of his reforming friend, at a time when Luther was looked upon even by his friends as too aggressive, too revolutionary, and too dangerous. Apparently most of his friends at Wittenberg looked upon Luther as a bright star, but they saw the implications of his ideas in sermons and biblical studies, and some were very cautious about becoming followers. Not so with Spalatin, however, for he gave enthusiastic support at every point, including not only matters of scholarly theological concern, but in the practical matters of salaries for colleagues and other everyday concerns in administering a fledgling University, as well as in the organizational development of the Reformation.

Upon occasion Spalatin could not defend his friend, for Luther was not always diplomatic in his requests and actions. The Friar of Wittenberg seemed to feel that the Elector and the other princes needed his bull-in-the-china-shop approach. Melanchthon tried to soften the approach in some important theological disputes and ecclesiastical matters, but Spalatin was the real link between Luther and the civil authorities with the Elector Frederick, and with the other electoral princes.

In the period immediately preceding the Diet of Worms in 1521, Jean Glaupion, the confessor to the Emperor Charles V, got in touch with Spalatin, seeking to find some basis for conciliation. He wanted to avoid a head-on conflict between Luther and the Church. The Diet was not really called to deal with the fractious monk, but he had become the burning issue. Glaupion was not opposed to all of Luther's early teachings and writings but felt that "the Babylonian Captivity of the Church" was excessively harsh, and said he, personally, felt "scourged and pummeled from head to foot."

Luther's safe-conduct to Worms, negotiated by Spalatin, was not the first such arrangement granted to Luther through the good offices of the Elector. Before going to Augsburg in 1518, Luther had been threatened with extradition to Italy to face Pope Leo. Uncertain of his chances of survival after such a confrontation, and given his most recent writings and the posting of the Ninety-five Theses and the likelihood that the least he would suffer would be finding himself silenced and kept in Rome, Luther wrote to Spalatin proposing that the German Princes should not allow their subjects to be forcibly taken to Italy. The Elector Frederick accepted Luther's proposition, largely because he felt that Luther had been good for the University of Wittenberg—and probably as a matter of exercising political clout with Emperor Maximilian. The Emperor, soon to be succeeded by Charles V, may have thought of Luther as politically important in his dealings with the Holy See, telling the Elector to "take good care" of Martin Luther.

Maximilian set an Imperial Diet for October 12–14, 1518, at Augsburg, and Pope Leo X elected to put aside his plan to bring Luther to Rome in favor of having him examined by Cardinal Cajetan. Cajetan was instructed to offer Luther full pardon, and there is some evidence that he also offered future preferment in the Church, if the recalcitrant monk would submit to the authority of the Church. Luther went to the Diet under imperial safe-conduct, expecting the worst. He was only a lone Augustinian monk who was accused of heresy and opposed by the Emperor, a Cardinal, and the Pope.

The Elector Frederick was frequently offended by the ideas preached and written by Luther. He thought that Luther was unnecessarily and immoderately crude in his writings. But he was not called "The Wise" for nothing. His judgments were humane and were based upon common sense and a weighing of values, with a well-honed understanding of men and motives.

In all his dealings with Luther, Frederick depended on Spalatin for advice and counsel. In a very real sense, Spalatin was not only a secretary but a confidant, one to whom the Elector could go, and upon whom he could depend for reasonable understanding and clarification. Because Spalatin had from the beginning hitched himself to the star that was Martin Luther, their friendship brought huge dividends of support from the Elector Frederick and his successors in the princely office over several decades.

Spalatin was involved in Luther's relationship with numerous others of his friends, since Martin so often approached the Elector on their behalf. So, Spalatin was the go-between in the negotiations that resulted in Melanchthon being called to the faculty at Wittenberg, although Luther favored the appointment of Peter Mosellaneous, a Greek scholar from Leipzig. The Elector made the decision, then delegated Spalatin to meet the new young professor in Augsburg and escort him to Wittenberg. After Melanchthon began his teaching at the University, Luther and Spalatin were quick to realize his abilities, and their appreciation became the subject of much correspondence between them. Just two days after Philipp's first lecture, Luther wrote to Spalatin that "we now no longer wonder why you commend him to us."

Several days later, Luther wrote to Spalatin, sympathizing with the Elector, whose problems Spalatin had mentioned. Some of the problems related to the administration of the University. Martin had suggested that some of the traditional courses be made optional, telling his friend how the students were crowding the lecture hall to hear Melanchthon. Luther wanted more courses on the Bible and "real" theology, with less of Aristotle and the scholastic theologians. Spalatin encouraged Luther, indicating that the Elector was pleased with the progress of the University, and suggesting that Luther might be elevated to bishop because of his fine work and growing influence.

In the course of letters like these, Luther expressed himself freely on churchmen, civil authorities, and ordinary events of the day, as well as the progress of various reforms. One of the ignition points of the Reformation was the selling of indulgences, which offered remission from time in purgatory and eternal punishment in return for payment of sums for the building of St. Peter's in Rome. Luther wrote to Spalatin on the ethical and theological wrongness of the indulgence theory and expressed his frank opinions about those who were selling them. He had come to the point in his thinking by early 1518 that he could write to Spalatin, "Indulgences now seem to me to be nothing but a snare for souls, and are worth absolutely nothing except to those who slumber and idle in the way of Christ."

The Ninety-five Theses were kind of a compendium of Luther's thinking about the abuses of Rome, and especially about indulgences and the papal arrogance that promoted them, and were a public indication of how far Luther had gone in his own reform thinking. In his letters to Spalatin he gave clear indication that the Ninety-five Theses were just the starting point of his challenge of papal power. In 1519, after dealing with Miltitz, and after writing a letter of submission on March 3, Luther wrote a letter to Spalatin ten days later (March 13) in which he gave vent to his true feelings about the Pope— any Pope, really: "I am at a loss to know whether the Pope is Antichrist or his apostle." While this was a major charge against the Pope, the language was mild compared to what he wrote to Spalatin about other individuals. Apparently, he felt secure in their friendship, and that, therefore, he could express himself honestly, knowing that Spalatin would keep his confidence.

Spalatin, throughout his career, maintained a cordial relationship with the great Dutch scholar Erasmus, as did Melanchthon, John Lang, and Justus Jonas. He occasionally heard from Luther about the shortcomings of Erasmus, as in 1516 when Luther wrote that his real problem with Erasmus was that, in spite of his biblical studies, the Dutchman seemed to be quite unaware of St. Paul's teachings on sin. He also wrote that Erasmus seemed equally unaware of Augustinian theology, apparently preferring Jerome to Augustine. Obviously, Luther would have none of this. Luther's relationship to Erasmus was maintained through Spalatin carrying such ideas back and forth.

One can trace the evolution of Luther, the Reformer, in his letters to Spalatin. Luther moved from one conclusion to another, following what seemed to him logical reasoning. From being an obedient and submissive son of the Church, he gradually began to realize where his thinking was taking him. His constant correspondence with Spalatin was a clarifying agent in his personal thought, until he gradually knew that he was indeed breaking away from the Church. In expressing his criticisms to Spalatin, it's almost as if he were trying on his thoughts for size. In 1517, after posting the Theses, he wrote: "It was the love of truth that drove me to enter this labyrinth and stir up six hundred minotaurs." In the uproar that followed the Theses, many of those who had been friends of Luther cautiously began to distance themselves from him. When they, along with those who had opposed Luther from the beginning as an upstart monk, began to oppose what was at the heart of Luther's thinking and expression, he became more critical of them and the Church. Gradually, he came to the conclusion that the sticking point was papal authority, with all its abuses, present and potential. The day came when he knew, much to his own surprise—he that was so loyal to the true Church that he would dare to excommunicate the Pope—that he had gone beyond the point of no return and would not have anything further to do with Popery. This he immediately wrote to Spalatin.

Spalatin helped Luther in his relationship with the Elector Frederick, on the one hand by keeping the Elector informed about the Reformer's public activities, and on the other hand by coaching Luther in his approach to the Elector. Frederick was wise and reasonable in his approach to many delicate subjects, which meant that Luther had a fair hearing on ideas and proposals that were quite removed from the thinking of ordinary citizens as well as church authorities. The Elector had a substantial collection of relics and was not opposed to indulgences. For him they were practical matters of faith and practice. However, he was perceptive enough to know when they were being abused. Because he had a concern for truth as basic in his University, he was pleased when Spalatin told him of the plans Luther had for changes in the courses of study. And it didn't hurt Luther's cause that the changes he made led to the increasing enrollment in the University.

Sylvester Prierias, a papal inquisitor, published a criticism of Luther in 1517, intended as an answer to the Ninety-five Theses, calling it "Dialogue Against the Presumptuous Conclusions of Martin Luther." Luther felt the authorities in Rome were interested primarily in silencing him without seriously looking at what he had said and written. He answered the attack of Prierias with "Resolutions" in April 1518, sending copies to his own local bishop and to the Pope. He protested his loyalty to the Pope and to the Church but insisted on the superior nature of councils as opposed to papal authority, along with derogatory references to indulgences, relics, the merits of saints and other orthodoxies. Pope Leo X forthwith summoned Luther to Rome.

In this tense situation, Luther wrote to Spalatin: "I need your help more than ever. . . . You should use your influence with the Sovereign and Pfeffinger." He wanted the Elector, as the civil authority, and Pfeffinger, as the administrator of the University, to see that his case was tried in German before German judges. He indicated some of the animus against him may have been because he was an Augustinian and Prierias a Domincan. And he realized that Spalatin could come to the rescue. When it became known that the Pope had asked the Elector and the Emperor Maximilian to arrest Luther, his friends cast about for ways to protect him. Spalatin received a letter suggesting that the Elector should refuse a safe-conduct to Rome, giving Luther an excuse for not going. This became the background for Cajetan coming to Augsburg in 1518 to give Luther a chance to recant and to be restored to the good graces of the Pope and the Church.

Spalatin was more cautious in pushing Luther's theological and ecclesiological concepts. In spite of wondering where Luther was leading his growing group of followers, Spalatin favored the changes at almost every point and conveyed this to the Elector. His caution probably came out of his closeness to the Elector, and therefore his consciousness of the political and social, as well as religious implications of much that Luther proposed. Spalatin recognized how close Luther was coming to the position of Huss, for example, a position that was fraught with much danger, given the condemnation of Huss by the authorities and his being burned at the stake.

Therefore, it must have been a burden to him to hear from Luther in 1519, as he prepared for the Leipzig disputation with Eck: "We are all Hussites now. . . ." This came several years after Spalatin had raised questions about Luther preaching a series of sermons in 1516 on prayer to the saints being an abuse of prayer. Spalatin wrote then, asking whether Luther was not participating in the Hussite heresy. Martin responded that he was concerned only with the abuses, not with the practices themselves. He wanted people to pray to the saints, but for spiritual, not material, gain. Spalatin was more sensitive than Luther to the effect such preaching would have in places of authority, both civil and religious, and knew that Luther had been moving in this direction for over a year in his condemnation of corruption of the Church in his classes at he University. He did not protest too much because he knew that Luther was talking about abuses that were well-known within the Church.

Luther and Spalatin also exchanged letters on the matter of personal religious experiences. When he was writing and lecturing on the Psalms, Luther, knowing the value of the work of the Dominican mystic John Tauler (1290-1361), urged Spalatin: "Get yourself the sermons of Johann Tauler" and enclosed a copy of "A German Theology," which Luther said came from the heart and pen of Tauler. "Take it and see how sweet is the Lord after you have first tried and realized how bitter is whatever we are." Sharing his enthusiasm for the religious insight of Tauler with his friend was a typical gesture on the part of Luther.

And, through Spalatin Luther wanted to share his faith understandings with his Prince. In 1519, the court feared for the Elector's life as he suffered through agonizing bouts with kidney stones, gout, and fever. Spalatin thought Luther could offer spiritual comfort and asked him to write to the Elector.

George Spalatin.

Within a month, the Reformer produced a small book of spiritual counsel, *The Fourteen of Consolation for Those Who Labor and Are Heavy Laden*, sending it to Spalatin in manuscript form in Latin, asking him to translate it into German for the benefit of the Elector. Later it was published and given general circulation. The "Fourteen" were seven evils and their counterparts in seven blessings, based on Luther's own gradual acceptance of the doctrine of justification by faith. The Elector evidently found "consolation" in the writing, and his support of Luther was reinforced.

When Melanchthon posted a notice on the bulletin board announcing the bonfire to burn the books of those critical of and opposed to Luther, the Reformer decided to burn the Papal Bull,

Exsurge Domine, as a way of countering what he thought to be the unreasonable and unscriptural attacks directed at him. They had burned his books, he would burn theirs. This, of course, was not an act to be taken lightly. The Bull put him under threat as well as others foolish enough to join him or support him in any way. To burn the Bull was to add insult to injury to the Church authorities, especially the Pope. It was an attack not only on Papal powers, but canon law as well. And the canon law was to a large degree the fabric of Luther's society. Luther probably felt a certain security, not only in his assumption that he was right, but also in the fact that the Elector was in his corner. When Luther wrote a pamphlet in answer to the Bull, "Ground and Reason for All the Articles Wrongly Condemned by the Roman Bully," Spalatin assured him he could publish it. When Luther told his friend that he was of a mind to burn the Papal Bull, Spalatin consulted with the Elector and the response quickly came: Burn not only the Bull but papal decrees and canon law as well. The Elector was probably expressing himself as Prince, not as believer.

Spalatin also served as Luther's go-between with Erasmus. At first Luther was open to the opinions and possible support of the great Dutch scholar, but he gradually came to the conclusion that those who were not really for him were really against him. Erasmus came under this judgment but kept an open mind on Martin Luther in most instances. Spalatin kept up a friendly correspondence with Erasmus, seeking his judgments and passing on to him what Luther was thinking.

In 1516, Luther lectured on Galatians, using Erasmus's Greek edition of the New Testament. However, he objected to Erasmus's commentaries on the New Testament and wrote to Spalatin about his objections. Luther referred to Erasmus as "the most learned man," but took issue with the learned man's understanding of St. Paul, saying the righteousness found in "works" or the "law" was not just in ceremonial observances. To Luther, the law meant the whole of God's moral law as well as the laws of society. The law is necessary for society, but we are not able to completely obey it, or we only try to obey it in a formal and superficial way. Christ offers grace that enables us to fulfill the law and to be reconciled in Christ, who bears our sins. To Luther, Erasmus failed to understand the real force and dignity of the law. Luther wrote to Spalatin, asking him to pass this criticism on to Erasmus.

Through Spalatin, Erasmus confirmed for Frederick the truth of the charges made by Luther about corruption in the Church and the soundness of Luther's theological prescriptions. Being the Elector's trusted adviser, Spalatin was the channel by which Luther was able to gain the Elector's support, and to assure him of the intellectual and biblical respectability of Luther's work.

So, in 1519, Luther wrote to Spalatin, in order to reach the Elector Frederick, "The Roman decrees must allow me full liberty to the true Gospel." And on July 20, 1520, "If they did not confute us on reasonable grounds and by written proof, but proceed against us by force and censures, then things will become twice as bad in Germany as in Bohemia." Luther went on to argue that the Elector, not knowing whether Luther was guilty or not, should not be hasty in making judgments. The letter was written to Spalatin, but the Elector was persuaded completely and wrote to Rome to suggest that until Luther could be instructed by Holy Scripture, no one could reasonably reproach him.

Spalatin was called upon not only to keep his Prince in Luther's corner, but to share in such activities as the translation of the Bible. Although Melanchthon was Luther's chief collaborator in the translation, Spalatin and others sat in with them in many consultations as the work progressed. Luther, while at the Wartburg working on the New Testament, wrote to Spalatin, "Philipp and I have now begun to correct the translation of the New Testament; it will, please God, turn out to be a fine work. We shall need your help here and there for a choice of words; hence, get ready." It is interesting to note, in passing, that Luther is credited with the development of the modern German language through his translation of the Bible into "the common German language so that both the upper and lower lands can understand me," yet he called upon Spalatin for "a choice of words." He specifically asked for the German names of the precious stones mentioned in the Book of Revelation. He wanted the translation to be a "homely one" with simple words, not the language of the men at arms or of the court. Luther was finding it difficult, as he put it, to "cram Hebrew writers into a German mould," but he was bound that he was going to "look into the jaws" of the man in the street in order to provide a Bible for everyone—men and women, those of both high and low estate. Cochleus reports that shoemakers and women became Bible students, so well-read that they were able to carry on conversations about it with doctors of theology.

Spalatin also was a major factor in Luther's appearance before the triennial chapter meeting of the Augustinian Congregation in Heidelberg (1518), the confrontation with Cajetan at Augsburg (1518), dealing with Milit14 (1519), the disputation with Eck at Leipzig (1519), the burning of the Papal Bull (1520), the Diet of Worms (1521), and the "kidnapping" and safe-keeping that followed. Add to these the Bible translations, the Peasants' Revolt, the Diets of Speier and Augsburg, and the development of the Reformation Churches.

Although Melanchthon, Jonas, Bugenhagen, and Amsdorf were close personal friends and neighbors to Luther, no one was closer to him than Spalatin in the day-to-day, almost hour-by-hour unfolding of the Reformation.

When Luther went to Heidelberg for the Chapter meeting in April-May 1518, he obtained through Spalatin the Elector's permission to take leave from the University. Luther was finishing his stint as district Vicar of the Augustinians, serving under his old friend and mentor, Johann von Staupitz, the Vicar-General. Probably the tension generated with the Dominicans by Luther's criticism of Tetzel's sale of indulgences helped the Elector agree to the professor's absence. The Dominicans had commented unfavorably on the University of Wittenberg harboring a suspected heretic, which implied a criticism of the Elector. There was some suggestion that if the monk got outside of Saxony, he would be apprehended by the local authorities, and given short shrift for his dereliction.

The Elector, indicating Luther would have his protection, gave him permission to leave his classes, and gave him letters of introduction to persons of consequence, both along his route and in Heidelberg. Spalatin suggested that he travel in disguise, but Luther preferred not to take advantage of his safe-conduct or any disguise, insisting instead on his trust in God. From the chapter meeting, Luther wrote to his friend, telling him what a happy experience he had, including rather handsome entertainment by the Count Palatine at the Heidelberg Castle. The meeting was a triumph for Luther and the emerging Reformation theology, so much so that Staupitz suggested that his former pupil should return home by wagon, paid for by the Augustinians.

On January 3, 1519, Luther met with Karl von Miltitz at the home of Spalatin in Altenburg in an attempt to bring together the diverging views of the Pope, himself, and the Elector. The Elector was not present but was represented by his secretary,

George Spalatin. Miltitz was authorized to offer the gift of a Golden Rose to Frederick the Wise, a signal honor conferred by the Pope on one prince each year. He also suggested that Pope Leo X favored the selection of Frederick to be Emperor, rather than Francis of France or Charles of Spain. In addition, those who made suitable contributions to the Castle Church of Wittenburg would have their time in purgatory reduced by one hundred years for each bone in the Elector's collection of relics. All this indicated that the Pope was in a mood for strategic conciliation when Miltitz met with Spalatin to discuss the matter of Martin Luther. One Cardinal is reported to have told Miltitz, "You are a pack of fools if you think you can buy the monk from the prince." Before Luther joined Miltitz and Spalatin, the Elector Frederick had received letters from papal authorities referring to him as "that child of Satan, son of perdition, scrofulous sheep, and tare in the vineyard, Martin Luther."

The upshot was that Martin arrived in Altenburg and sat with Miltitz and Spalatin, but the Pope's representative made no headway in his mission. Apparently the meeting was, at least on the face of it, cordial. Miltitz was cautious in his approach, having taken his own straw poll as he moved through Germany, and finding that half the country was hostile to Rome, and that three out of four citizens were supporters of the recalcitrant monk. Martin agreed to write a letter of submission to the Pope. Matters of division were to be left to a future meeting between Luther and papal representatives. Luther evidently was not completely won over by Miltitz, for he wrote much later that he had a suspicion that Miltitz was playing a part. He described the Legate's tears at their parting as "crocodile tears."

Spalatin did not join Luther in the debate with Eck at Leipzig, June 27–July 14, 1519, for he was busy with the Elector in Frankfurt-am-Main where a new Emperor was being elected. But they were in constant correspondence, as usual. And after the Leipzig Disputation where the issue was clearly defined, not as indulgences but as papal authority, Luther gave a full account to Spalatin. There followed considerable correspondence between the Elector, the new Emperor, Charles V, and the Pope concerning the coming Diet of Worms, the first of several Diets called by Charles to try and solve some of the problems of the empire. On behalf of the Elector, Spalatin sought the best possible terms under which Luther would come to the Diet, including safe-conduct to and from Worms, the manner of presentation of any charges, and guarantees of Luther's right to public reply.

Luther engaged in a barrage of printed material in 1520, some of it self-initiated, some in response to attacks by Eck, Aleander and others. Pope Leo X issued the Bull Exsurge Domine on June 15, 1520, condemning some forty-one statements of Luther, ordering public burning of many of the monk's writings, and ordering Luther to acknowledge his errors. If he refused to go to Rome to recant, after sixty days he would be excommunicated. All secular authorities were to banish him and deliver him to Rome. Luther forthwith wrote—in German to demonstrate his German nationalism—a series of three short books which were a systematic statement of his position vis-a-vis the Church of Rome.

First came "An Open Letter to the Christian Nobility of the German Nation Concerning the Reform of the Christian Estates." When Aleander and Eck published the Papal Bull in Germany, Luther wrote "The Babylonian Captivity of the Church." Miltitz, still thinking a reconciliation possible, had persuaded Luther to write to Pope Leo with a modestly put claim for reform. The letter was sent, but in it he wrote as a pastor guiding an errant parishioner and included the third of his public declarations, "A Treatise on Christian Liberty." In the meantime, Aleander and

Eck were bringing back into line the churches in Miessen, Merseburg, and Brandenburg and seeing to the burning of Luther's books in Mainz, Cologne, and Louvain. Melanchthon and Luther then called for the retaliatory burning of Catholic books and the Papal Bull in Wittenberg.

Luther's writings and his actions had the support of his friends and students in Wittenberg, as well as of many peasant householders throughout Germany, especially in Saxony. This included the support of the Elector, urged by Spalatin. Rather than pick up Luther and send him to Rome, the Elector moved to assure Luther of his right to speak out and write whatever he was moved to by Scripture.

As we have seen, Luther's letter to the Pope did little to resolve the conflict between Luther and Rome, the failure of the meeting with Miltitz and the writing of the letter to Leo only setting the stage for the eventual confrontation at the Diet of Worms.

Spalatin was at Worms, engaged in many endeavors with the Elector in seeking a fair hearing for Luther. With others of the Elector's counselors he negotiated with representatives of the Church as well as those of the Emperor, Charles V. Charles was newly elected; he was only twenty years old and had no reputation for decision-making. He was constrained to support the Bull excommunicating Luther and to issue an edict against the monk and any who followed him. In spite of this, he was persuaded by Frederick, who was the most formidable of the princes, to offer safe-conduct to Luther to get him to Worms to be examined with regard to his supposed heresies.

Luther gave ample reason to require safe-conduct by his increasingly vitriolic expression about the activity of the Church in Germany, writing to Spalatin in June 1520, after receiving support from Melanchthon, Ulrich von Hutten,

Carlstadt, and Franz von Sickengen. He wrote: "I have cast the die. I now despise the rage of the Romans as much as I do their favor. I will not reconcile myself to them for all eternity. . . . Let them condemn and burn all that belongs to me; in return I will do as much for them. . . . Now I no longer fear, and am publishing a book in the German tongue about Christian reform, directed against the Pope, in language as violent as if I were addressing Antichrist." The book was the *Address to the Christian Nobility*, charging that the people of Germany had been and were wronged and oppressed by the Church of Rome, challenging papal authority and insisting that secular authorities had the right to be involved in religious affairs since all classes are spiritual.

The Elector and his chaplain prevailed, and safe-conduct was provided by the Emperor. The appearance of Luther at Worms, with his ringing defense, "Here I stand . . ." and his refusal to recant unless convinced by Scripture, led the friends of the embattled monk to fear for his life, safe-conduct or no. Without giving away their plans, the Elector and Spalatin had let Luther know that plans were laid to kidnap him after the Diet. Spalatin had been with Luther at the lodgings of the Archbishop of Trier, who tried for a last-minute persuasion of Martin to recant. The two left the Archbishop's house, visited with one of the Elector's counselors who had become ill at Worms, and returned to Luther's lodgings. There, representatives of the Emperor told Luther he would have just twenty-one days to get back to Wittenberg, after which the safe-conduct would expire.

On the return journey, Schurff, Jonas, and others journeyed with Luther as far as Mohra. Only Luther's brother James and Nicolas von Amsdorf accompanied him as he went on. Amsdorf was not totally unaware of the plot to kidnap Luther and was, therefore, not taken by surprise—as was the Reformer—when five men appeared as they went through the woods, and spirited Luther away. Brother James ran for his life. Amsdorf went on to Wittenberg to report the incident. Luther was taken to the Wartburg, a castle near Eisenach, where he disguised himself as Knight George, grew a beard, and a head of hair replacing his tonsure. He was kept in safety for almost a year before going back to Wittenberg to carry on his work.

Many of his followers feared for Luther's life during this time. They did not believe that a lone monk could challenge the Church and the power of the civil authorities who supported the Church in its authority stance. The Edict of Worms, actually issued about the time of the kidnapping, threatened not only the monk, but anyone who gave support to him. The fear which his friends had for his safety was symbolized in a letter written by Albrecht Dürer, the great artist, to Spalatin in 1520, some time before the Edict had concentrated the pressure and the danger: "If God helps me I will go to Doctor Martin Luther and make his likeness in copper for a lasting memorial for the Christian man who has helped me out of my anguish." Dürer's portrait of Luther still exists, and indeed it has been a lasting memorial to the Reformer.

Fear for Luther's safety intensified. Erasmus was asked by the Elector Frederick for his advice concerning the affair of Luther, and replied, "I am not at all astonished that he has occasioned such a hubbub, for he has committed two unpardonable faults, which consist of having attacked the triple crown of the Pope and the belly of the monks." This was, of course, only a humorous way of describing the reasons for the danger that Luther brought upon himself, criticizing the Church and its place in the German states of the sixteenth century. The response of the Church was to threaten Luther, and the experience of

Huss and other condemned heretics suggested how serious the threats could be.

During this time Luther was in almost daily contact with Spalatin, not only for the intellectual and personal support he received, but because Spalatin was the key to the Elector's continuing support and defense. And Spalatin was completely devoted to Luther and the Reformation.

In his frequent letters to Spalatin, Luther expressed his dependence upon his friends, including the Elector, for his safety, and for their important place in the work of reform especially in the event of his being cut off by death or imprisonment. He needed their support and friendship. When Luther was summoned to Worms, he wrote to Spalatin, "I will do what in me lies, to be carried there sick, if I cannot go well. . . . Expect anything except flight or recantation." From the Wartburg he wrote, "What is going on in the world I care nothing for. Here I sit in quiet." Spalatin replied, in view of the excesses of Carlstadt and Müntzer—priests marrying, monks and nuns leaving the cloisters and marrying, meat on feast days, the Mass in German and in both kinds, images and statues defaced—"What a mess we are in!"

The mess was not enough, nor the pressures great enough to separate the two men, for Luther had shared with Spalatin his most personal thinking on such matters as the marriage of priests, monks, and nuns. While Luther was at the Wartburg, Carlstadt not only damaged the Reform Movement by his iconoclastic actions, but married a fifteen-year-old girl as well. Luther approved of the marriage, although he wrote to Spalatin, "Good Heavens! Will our Wittenbergers give wives to monks?" But he for some time had been edging closer to the idea that the monastic vows of celibacy were very questionable. Now he wrote a tract, "On Monastic Vows," which he sent first to Spalatin, who delayed publication because of its frankness. Luther's thesis was that the vows of celibacy countered a natural God-inspired sexual instinct, and therefore monastic vows were a lure of Satan, multiplying sins. Both he and Spalatin were subsequently married.

The correspondence of the two friends with regard to the marriage of nuns was typical of many of their exchanges. The Reformer had been receiving nuns at his quarters in the Black Cloister, many of whom married churchmen. In April 1523 nine escaping nuns were brought to him by Leonard Koppe and his nephew, Wolf Tomitzsch. Over a period of months, matches were made for most of them, or homes were found with friends and families. Martin wrote to Spalatin upon their arrival, "Grace and peace. Nine fugitive nuns, a wretched crowd, have been brought to me. You ask what I shall do with them? First I shall inform their relatives, and ask them to support the girls. . . . For some I shall get husbands if I can . . . beg some money from your rich courtiers, by which I can support the girls for a week or two until their kinsmen or others provide for them." Later, in 1525, Luther wrote to Spalatin, and raging—jokingly we presume—that it was strange that "a famous lover like me does not get married." After referring to nuns who have helped him in his bachelor's quarters, he continues, "I have had three wives simultaneously . . . but you are a sluggish lover who does not dare to become a husband of even one woman. Watch out that I, who have no thought of marriage at all, do not one day overtake you." After Spalatin married, Luther wrote to him proposing that on an appointed night they make love to their respective wives and think of one another—which is pushing the concept of collegiality pretty far!

When the Elector died, although he had never left the Roman Catholic Church, on his deathbed he received holy

Memorial church at Speyer, Germany, commemorating the "protest" of the princes which gave the name "Protestant" to the Reformation.

communion "in both kinds," both bread and wine. Luther and Melanchthon conducted the funeral services, and the burial was in the Castle Church in Wittenberg, without the Catholic ritual. Credit is given, as it should be, to the Elector Frederick for his steadfast support of Luther; much of the reason for this support, however, was the constant influence of George Spalatin.

The death of Frederick the Wise was a great blow to Spalatin. Both Luther and Melanchthon praised the Elector for his efforts to keep the peace and for his support of them personally. They knew how great a work the Elector had done, primarily through his secretary/chaplain, Spalatin.

Frederick's death meant a change in Spalatin's life. After some three and a half months he became pastor of St. Bartholomew's Church in Altenburg, a small town some forty miles south of Leipzig. There he served as pastor, all the while continuing correspondence with Luther to the time of his (Spalatin's) death in 1545, carrying on an important work of visitation among the churches, and building up the work of Christian education in the Reformation churches. He was also a trusted adviser to Electors John the Steadfast and John Frederick, successors to Frederick the Wise.

At every major confrontation of Luther with the world and the Church from 1517–1545, Spalatin was either at his side or in constant communication with him. At the Diet of Speyer in 1529, remembered as the scene of the "protest" of the Lutheran princes which gave the name to "Protestants," Spalatin was an adviser to the princes as well as to Luther. The next year, at the Diet of Augsburg, he helped in the framing of the Augsburg Confession, written by Melanchthon but approved by reform leaders. After the Elector Frederick, the Margrave George and Landgrave Philip had refused to kneel before the Emperor and papal representative. Spalatin and Melanchthon were up all night developing a statement on why the Protestant princes could not participate in the Corpus Christi procession the following day. They believed the elevation of the Host in the procession to be idolatry. Luther was not at Augsburg, but he wrote to Spalatin to keep him up with what was going on, and Spalatin likewise kept him apprised of what was happening.

By 1537 the Catholic and Protestant division was so marked that the Protestant princes refused the Pope's invitation to attend the Council of Mantua. Instead they met at Schmalkalden and asked Luther to present a statement representing the position of the evangelicals. Luther felt that, rather than proposing toleration of the Protestant position, he should show his open hostility to papal power in view of its continuing corruption. He was joined in this position by his colleagues who gathered at Wittenberg to give their approval. Included were Justus Jonas, Cruciger, Bugenhagen, Agricola, Amsdorf, and, of course, Spalatin. Called the Schmalkald Articles, the statement was sent to the Elector John the Constant who gave his complete approval. (Along with the Augsburg Confession these articles are reckoned among the basic documents of Lutheran churches throughout the world.)

In 1539, when Luther told people the best way to study theology, he remembered a very early (1519) letter to Spalatin: "Despair of your reason and understanding. Kneel down in your little room and pray to God with real humility and earnestness that he through his dear Son may give you his Holy Spirit, who will enlighten you, lead you, and give you understanding."

When Spalatin died in 1545 at the age of sixty, he had been involved for about thirty-three years with the Friar of Wittenberg. He had become a convinced and devoted colleague very early, and stayed late. As Luther's key to the support, influence, and material resources of the Electors Frederick the Wise, John the Constant, and John Frederick, Spalatin was a crucial figure in the Reformation. He was an intelligent, capable, energetic person who lent himself totally to his friend Martin Luther. The cautions he sometimes expressed were those of one who understood the political realities of Luther's world and wanted to spare him the pitfalls. It is probably not too far off the mark to say that the Reformation could not have been as effective as it was without George Spalatin, one of Luther's best friends.

CHAPTER 9

Frederick the Wise

When seeing the older sections of Leipzig, Coburg, Wittenberg, Worms, and other cities and towns that figure so prominently in the German Reformation, it is difficult to put events and persons in their place. Traveling in modern style at modern speeds, it is hard to visualize great events in such modest settings and occurring at such a slow pace. In a couple of hours you can move from Leipzig to Wittenberg to Erfurt to Eisenach. Go in another direction and three or four hours take you from Wittenberg to Augsburg to Speyer. Martin Luther went by ox-cart or carriage, by horseback or shanks mare. His cause gave him strength and persistence, but sometimes he had to confess weariness, and he succumbed with increasing frequency to debilitating illness and physical exhaustion.

Luther's friends saw what was happening and urged him to slow down, to eat better and to sleep more, to avoid some of the confrontations that took so much out of him. But he persisted.

Among those who sometimes made life easier for the Reformer was his Prince, the Elector Frederick the Wise—one of the seven prince-electors who represented the German states in the election of the Holy Roman Emperor. The acknowledged leader of the German princes, Frederick was a man of great wealth and power who controlled the secular state of Saxony and its ecclesiastical and theological life as well. From time to time, for reasons of state, he eased Luther's life, providing travel accommodations and protection, aid for his friends and supporters, a lovely place for Luther's family residence, and, with some regularity, game and wine for his table.

Luther also was supported and his cause advanced by a number of city and regional rulers. Germany of the sixteenth century was divided into many municipalities, principalities, dukedoms, and other civilian and Church domains. Of all these rulers, Frederick the Wise was by far the most important and influential. He was born in Torgau, January 17, 1463. In 1486 he succeeded his father, Ernest, as Elector of Saxony. Torgau was not by any means a metropolitan center, but it was the site of one of several castles that the electors of Saxony called home. It was the chief castle of the Ernestine Saxon rulers. Others of their castles were at Coburg and the Wartburg at Eisenach, in both of which Luther found refuge when he was in trouble.

In 1485, when Frederick was twenty-two years old, the lands controlled by the House of Wettin were divided into two sections, following a dispute in the family: one, including Dresden and Leipzig, was given to the younger son, Albert, who took the title of Duke, with his domain being Albertine, or Ducal Saxony; the other, larger but poorer Saxony, became the property of Ernest, older brother of Albert, and was designated as Ernestine or Electoral Saxony, with Ernest as Imperial Elector. The following year Ernest died, and Frederick became the Prince-Elector, continuing as such until his death in 1525. He soon established himself as a leader among the German princes, who called him "the Wise."

Frederick remained a Roman Catholic throughout his life, having one of the most extensive and well-known collections of relics in Christendom. He restored the Castle Church at Wittenberg, All Saints, primarily to house his collection of relics. The town was noted by Luther as a "miserable place," but soon became a place of pilgrimage as the faithful were drawn to view the relics, with indulgences being awarded for viewing them. After accession to the Electorate, Frederick made a pilgrimage to Jerusalem, along the way scouring Europe and the Near East for relics. By 1509, over 5000 items were on hand, including scraps of hay from the true manger, part of the cradle of the infant Jesus, the swaddling clothes, fragments of the true cross, as well as many other items offered for veneration. In spite of Luther's description of Wittenberg—"on the confines of civilization . . . mean in appearance and insignificant among German cities"—it became the preeminent place of pilgrimage in all of Northern Germany, with people often coming great distances to give evidence of their faith.

The collection of relics was the pride and joy of the Elector, who continued to add to it to his last days, there being finally over 19,000 items. Not only did Frederick believe in the efficacy of veneration of relics, he also believed in the efficacy of indulgences. He arranged for indulgences to be offered through viewing his relics and allowed their sale for the building of a bridge over the Elbe River at Torgau for which he hired the monk Tetzel. Tetzel later became notorious for selling indulgences and raising the hackles of another monk, Martin Luther. The Elector also permitted the sale of indulgences in 1502 to raise funds for a crusade against the Turks, who at that time were a threat against Christian Europe. When the crusade did not happen, he withheld the funds, and these were the funds he used to found a University at Wittenberg.

When Tetzel came selling indulgences in 1517 for the proposed rebuilding of St. Peter's Cathedral in Rome, the Elector decided that too much money was going out of Germany and forbade his coming into Saxony. Tetzel set up shop just across the border, and the people found it easy to cross over and buy indulgences. Some took them to the young monk, Martin Luther, for his appraisal as to whether they were really of value in getting to heaven. Their questions focused Luther's thinking, and the result was the nailing of Ninety-five Theses to the Castle Church door in Wittenberg, October 31, 1517. The next day, All Saints Day, the Elector's collection of relics was to be on display, with a large crowd expected. Ironically, Luther began his movement of reform challenging his benefactor's most cherished concerns. The Augustinian monk didn't realize that he was starting a revolution; he thought he was only being faithful to his Church and seeking to preserve it from abuse. The Elector too became convinced of this by his secretary, George Spalatin, who had been attracted to Luther very early and who was Luther's access to the Elector and to the Elector's successors throughout his life.

Luther criticized indulgences because they put the believer's faith in jeopardy. Indulgences led Christians to believe that they could buy their way into heaven. The Elector did not want to see so much money go to Rome, being mindful that Germany was called the "milch cow of the papacy," and of the accusation that the Pope got more revenue from Germany than was received by the German princes. So Frederick refused to relax his opposition to the indulgences even for the Archbishop of Mainz, one of his good friends. His reasons were political and economic, however, not theological or spiritual.

In 1512, Luther was teaching at the University Frederick the Wise had founded at Wittenberg. It soon became one of the better known in the sixteenth century, joining a list that included such well-known universities as those in Prague, Vienna, Geneva, Erfurt, Heidelberg, Louvain, Ingolstadt, Copenhagen, Uppsala, and Leipzig. Most of the European universities remained loyal to the Roman Catholic Church as the Reformation progressed, with the most significant exceptions being Erfurt, Wittenberg, and Jena. Luther studied at Erfurt, taught at Wittenberg, and his theology was defended most effectively after his death in the establishment of the University of Jena.

Frederick was a political, not a theological person. Many times he supported Luther against not only the Church and the Emperor, but also among his own electoral peers; not for theological reasons however; Luther's abilities impressed him. He was concerned that the young professor expound the Scriptures in good conscience. Frederick was also motivated by growing nationalist consciousness. He was one of the first to sense, and to seek to direct, the growing German-ness of the German people. The schools he founded were aimed at establishing the German language and identity. Luther and Luther's Reformation were for him something to support and encourage because they fit into his scheme of things. Luther, especially in his Bible translations, continually aimed at making the Bible available and understandable to every German, in his language and his national idiom.

Along with his emphasis on German-ness in Bible translation was Luther's opportunistic approach to the idea of separation of Church and State. This, again, fit into the Elector's thinking. Luther saw the Church and the secular state as within God's creations, ordained by the Scriptures. In temporal affairs and secular concerns, Scripture—that is, God—put secular authorities in charge. In spiritual matters, concerns of faith, understanding of the Bible, the Scriptures put the Church in charge through its theologians and councils. Frederick opposed the idea of either Pope or emperor coming into Germany to tell him how to deal with church-state matters.

It is worth noting that Luther opposed the use of military force in the church and in the spiritual realm, preaching and writing that God did not want blood spilled for his purposes. In 1521, when the Zwickau prophets were a problem in Wittenberg with their revolutionary religious and civil proposals, the Elector had difficulty knowing how to handle the situation. Luther, from the Wartburg, wrote to Spalatin: "See that our Prince does not imbrue his hands in the blood of those new prophets of Zwickau." A couple of months later he wrote directly to the Elector: "In this business no sword can counsel or help; God must manage here alone, without any human care or aid." Yet, in the Peasants' War the Reformer came down heavily on the side of military force to stamp out the revolt and eliminate its leadership. His rationale was that this was a civil matter and God had ordained the princes to deal with civil concerns. The peasants violated scriptural law by revolting against the princes; therefore they must be restrained.

In a variety of situations, Luther spelled out his doctrine of "two realms" within the world, the temporal and the spiritual. He was constrained by Scripture to allow the Elector full power—subject to Biblical criticism, of course—in the business of civil, political, and economic organization. The religious life of the people and their rulers was the domain of the Church. Given the immense territorial and material wealth of the Church, there was considerable crossing of lines.

Frederick was convinced by Luther's reasoning, protecting him and saving him in several crucial situations. The Elector

Frederick the Wise.

was so persuaded by the monk, in fact, that he elected to defy the Emperor and the Church in providing security for Luther after he had been condemned by the interdiction of both Church and Emperor in the Papal Bull, Exsurge Domine, and the resulting excommunication. This was one of several times when a sort of quid pro quo pertained: the Elector intervened on Luther's behalf, and Luther provided justification from Scripture for the Elector's German nationalism, his cultural and political ambitions and convictions.

Frederick the Wise was very important in the imperial projections of Charles V. The Elector took the lead in voting for Charles, when he was chosen Emperor over Francis I, King of France. At first Pope Leo X had supported Francis but then switched to Charles and thereby assured his election. There is evidence that Charles was aided considerably in his election campaign by a large loan from the German banking family, the Fuggers, of Augsburg. Anton Fugger had loaned over one million florin to Charles, which translates into a huge sum even today.

As the indulgence controversy heated up and became ever more serious, Luther was commanded in 1518 to go to Rome to be examined for suspected heresy. The Elector refused to allow him to leave Germany, because he was not convinced that Luther had fallen into heresy. He covered himself in his defiance of the Church by insisting that, as a Christian prince, he would send his professor to Rome only if there was evidence brought forth to support the charges brought against him. Also, Frederick the Wise wanted to protect his fledgling University and its star professor.

The Elector found support for his protective stance in a letter from the great Dutch scholar, Desiderius Erasmus, who wrote that although he had read only certain parts of Luther's writings, anyone who was really concerned about religion would be sympathetic to him. "All who are conversant with his life," wrote Erasmus, "approved of it, since he was above every suspicion of ambition. The purity of his character is such that he wins over the heathen. No one has shown his error or refuted him, and yet they call him a heretic." With this he urged the Elector not to abandon Luther, since he was an innocent man.

Over the next few years Luther, in lectures, preaching, and writing became more and more critical of the Church, the Curia in Rome, the Pope and the papacy itself, the Archbishop of Mainz, the veneration of relics, and the governance of the Church. On occasion he expressed displeasure with the Elector when that worthy was involved with what he considered church malpractice. In some cases, the Elector refused to censure Luther, since he himself was of the opinion that the Church needed correction. Besides, all the criticisms came out of Luther's study of Scriptures and were based on biblical concept and precedent.

The Elector Frederick was called "the Wise" because of his good sense and fairness in decisions and was the most respected of the princes in Germany. When Maximilian died in 1519, it was originally proposed that Frederick be elected Emperor, but he rejected the idea, preferring to continue his role as leader of the Germans and loathe to become emperor and have to face conflict with the French and the Spanish. Aleander, one of several Papal Legates assigned to the German situation, referred to Frederick as "a fox." While decisive, he was cautious in his decisions and slow to change. But his concern for justice and truth led him to be open to conviction and fair-play. Because of his nationalist German feelings and his affection for his new University with its star theologian, Frederick was receptive to the recommendations of his secretary, Spalatin, who was constantly advancing the Reformer's interests.

As a consequence of the indulgence controversy, the Pope requested that Luther appear for questioning in Augsburg by the Pope's representative, Cardinal Cajetan. It was now 1518. Luther knew he was in danger. He wrote that he was "bereft of all human protection, of emperor, Pope, Cardinal Legate, my Prince Frederick, Duke of Saxony, my order, my closest friend, Staupitz." His Augustinian Vicar, Staupitz, suggested that he seek refuge elsewhere, perhaps in France. Luther, though, felt strongly that he should go to Augsburg, trusting in the safe-conduct assurances from the Elector, who had prevailed upon Cajetan to provide such assurances. The Elector had also given Luther a letter of introduction to friends who provided for him in Augsburg. The safe-conduct included travel through territories ruled by Duke George of Saxony—no friend of Luther even then—and Philip of Hesse, who as a very young man became a devoted follower of Luther. In Augsburg, Luther went to the

Carmelite monastery where an old friend, John Trosch, was prior. He had gone initially to the Augustinians but felt there was more safety with the Carmelites. Being assured once more of his personal safety, he met with Cardinal Cajetan on three successive days, October 10–13. Cajetan spoke in a cordial manner to Martin, but basically was only willing to hear a recantation of what Luther had been saying and writing. The Legate then wrote to the Elector, asking him to send Luther to Rome. After denunciating Luther as "one little monk" whose teachings were harmful to the Church, he demanded that the Elector expel Luther from Saxony, which would effectively remove him from the Elector's protection. Cajetan closed this letter with an appeal to Frederick's Catholic loyalty.

The Elector wrote to Cajetan at some length, reminding him that he had fulfilled his promise that Luther would personally appear before him in Augsburg, and that he was sure that the Cardinal would not condemn Luther without a full hearing on his case. He also called attention to the fact that many learned scholars did not think Luther heretical, that there was no reason to threaten action by the Roman Curia since Luther had not been convicted of heresy. He enclosed Luther's account of the meeting in this letter.

Following the Augsburg meeting and the exchange of letters which ran into December, the Pope took another approach. This time he sent a German nobleman, Charles von Miltitz, as his envoy to offer the Golden Rose to the Elector Frederick. This presentation was made each year to one of the princes, and was a signal mark of honor from the Pope. The envoy was to let the Elector know that he was to receive the Golden Rose but on condition that he do what the Pope wanted, which was to convince Luther to acknowledge the Pope's authority in the matter of indulgences. The real issue was not the indulgences, but papal authority. This meant that Frederick would either have to acknowledge Luther's heresy or deny the authority of the Pope. Miltitz also carried letters to Spalatin and Pfeffinger, a chief counselor, putting pressure on them to influence the Elector to abandon his loyalty to Luther.

In January 1519, Luther met with Miltitz at Altenburg. They had a cordial exchange which resulted in Luther making concessions—within his conscience—and Miltitz committing the Pope to a more generous approach. Martin agreed to go public with a statement that he was not trying to disgrace the Church and had been too zealous in his criticism. In addition, he agreed to write to the Pope. In his letter, he acknowledged the authority of the Pope, but his language made him seem like a father chastising the Pope. He also included a caveat, "if only my adversaries restrain their vain boasts." Generally, he seemed humble and contrite. Not too long after, he wrote to Spalatin a kind of renunciation of what he had written to the Pope, based on further reflection, and suggesting that the Pope was the Antichrist. The Elector was in constant communication with Luther in these weeks of conversation and correspondence.

Early in 1518, Frederick had received a letter from Cardinal Raphael Riario commanding him not to protect Luther's person or his writings. At Augsburg, Cajetan had asked him to send Luther to Rome. This the Elector refused to do, acceding to Luther's idea that German princes should protect German citizens from forced extradition to Rome. He was also impressed by the comment of the Emperor Maximilian, who, thinking perhaps of the religious tempest in Germany and its importance in any jousting with Rome, told the Elector to "take good care of that monk." Frederick did take care of that monk, refusing the demands of Riario on the basis that while he, the Elector, had never defended Luther's writings or sermons, Luther, it should be noted, had never refused to appear before "just, wise, and impartial judges to defend his doctrines, and if he should be taught better out of Holy Scripture, he would obediently submit."

The net result of the hearing in Augsburg was that the Elector Frederick emerged more clearly as the preeminent Prince-Elector of Germany and as Luther's friend and protector. He had been favorably disposed toward the Friar as monk and professor. Now he became, without surrendering his Roman Catholic credentials, the supporter of Luther and would have to be reckoned with in any attempt to get at the Reformer—this in spite of the fact that he still had had no personal contact with Luther. Everything was through intermediaries, with Luther as a kind of pawn in the power-politics of a nascent German nationalism.

When John Eck, an able theologian from the University of Ingolstadt, proposed a disputation with Luther's Wittenberg colleague, Carlstadt, the Elector supported the idea, believing that truth should be sought in every case. He also approved Luther going with Carlstadt, knowing that Carlstadt was arguing Luther's ideas, and that Luther should have a part in their exposition. Duke George also approved, and the debate was set for the Pleissenberg castle in Leipzig. Although Carlstadt later became one of Luther's enemies, he earned good marks from Luther for his demeanor at the Disputation.

After Carlstadt and Eck had debated for four days, Luther took up the challenge to the close of the disputation. He was seconded not only by Carlstadt, but more importantly by Philipp Melanchthon, the twenty-two-year-old theologian who recently had been recruited to teach Greek at the University of Wittenberg. The basic issue boiled down to that of papal authority, and, while Luther was not looked upon as the winner—if there could be one—the battle lines were drawn which were never later obliterated.

After a somewhat cordial relationship with Duke George at the Leipzig Disputation, Luther became *persona non grata* with the Duke by preaching a sermon in November 1519 in which he said that the Lord's Supper should be given to all men in both kinds, bread and wine, a Hussite idea toward which Luther had been moving. Duke George had been suspicious at Leipzig that Eck's charge that Luther was a Hussite was true. The Duke broke completely with Luther and advised his cousin, Frederick, to expel Luther from his portion of Saxony. The advice was not heeded but marked the point at which Luther lost all regard for the Duke toward whom he was, from then on, in open defiance.

When Luther, Melanchthon, and Carlstadt returned from Leipzig to Wittenberg in the autumn of 1519, Luther received word from Spalatin that the Elector was ill with gout, kidney stone, and fever and that he, Spalatin, thought that Luther should write something of spiritual consolation for his Prince. The Court in Torgau were afraid for his life. In about a month, Luther responded with "The Fourteen of Consolation For Those Who Labor and Are Heavy Laden," written in Latin, with a request that Spalatin make a free translation into German.

"The Fourteen" were seven evils and seven blessings, in contemplation of which the troubles of the Elector might be lightened. An accompanying letter suggested that this was intended as a kind of spiritual medicine. It was offered because "As far as I am concerned, being one whom Your Lordship's many benefits and signal benefactions have made your debtor before all other men, I acknowledge that I feel obliged to express my gratitude by performing some special service. Since by reason of my intellectual and material limitations I can offer nothing of value, I have welcomed the suggestion of your chaplain, Mr. George Spalatin, that I prepare some kind of spiritual consolation and present it to Your Lordship." The consolation Luther offered to the Elector was paralleled by his correspondence with those of low estate with troubles of every kind; in the case of the Elector it was a part of a long-standing relationship.

It was in this same year that Emperor Maximilian died, and Charles V of Spain was elected his successor as head of the Holy Roman Empire, including the German Nation. The Elector Frederick threw his weight, which included the weight of most of the German princes since he had been named administrator of the German empire, in favor of Charles V.

The Pope favored Francis I of France, but seeing where the power was, concurred with the German electors. The election and enthronement of the Emperor overshadowed other concerns, and for a time the pressure was taken off the affair of Luther and his possible heresies.

Luther's arguments at Leipzig gave substance to the Elector's growing feeling that Roman authority in matters religious and civil should not prevail in Germany. Erasmus concurred. In a letter to the Elector in April 1519, he wrote that "while it is the duty of your highness to protect the Christian religion, it is also your duty, inasmuch as you are the guardian of justice, not to permit an innocent man, under the pretence of piety, to be given up to the impiety of others." In May, Frederick replied, "I rejoice that the Lutheran cause is not condemned by the learned, and that with you Dr. Martin's writings are most eagerly read by the best men." He concluded by avowing his support of Luther, not because of his acceptance of the Lutheran teachings, but on the basis of justice: "By the help of God I will not permit an innocent man to be given up to the impiety of those who are seeking their own good in his ruin."

The Elector made a real effort to make known his loyalty to the Catholic faith, while insisting upon fairness and justice for his contentious monk. In 1520, with the Diet at Worms coming and Charles V seeking to consolidate his newly won position as Emperor, the Church was bringing more pressure on Luther. The Reformer wrote to Spalatin, obviously intending to get a message to the Elector concerning his appointment to the University and the apparent embarrassment this was causing: "Let his Highness the Prince put me out into the street so I may either be better instructed or confuted." He went on to say that he was willing to give up his position and belongings, but since the Elector himself is not qualified to bring instructive criticism, he should not judge or punish Luther until some true ecclesiastical conviction be imposed. The Prince "is in ignorance whether (anyone) be guilty or not . . . how then can the Romanists demand that he should step in and obey men rather than God?" Luther's letter persuaded the Elector, who then wrote to Rome that the monk was ready to be instructed by learned men from the Scriptures and that no one should reproach the Elector as disloyal to the faith of the Church and tolerating error. One of the reasons Charles V called the Diet at Worms was that he seemed to feel that Luther should not be condemned until he had been heard. His decision as a very young Emperor, just twenty, was perhaps also colored by the fact that he looked to Frederick as "Uncle" and was willing to accept his counsel.

The Emperor may have been willing to hear Luther out because of Frederick the Wise's constant reference to Scripture as a guide. Luther and Carlstadt had assured Frederick, in a letter after the Leipzig Disputation, that "a layman with Scripture on his side is more to be believed than the Pope and Council without Scripture." The appeal to Scripture as a standard of judgment, coupled with Luther's appeal to Frederick's Saxon Court on national grounds, not only made the Elector's support secure, but probably influenced the Emperor as well to at least not condemn the monk until he had been heard.

In the background was the issuing on June 15, 1520, of the Papal Bull, *Exsurge Domine,* which condemned forty-one propositions of Luther and gave him sixty days to recant. The idea of allowing sixty days before any excommunication should take place was due to Pope Leo X's hesitation to have any break with the Elector Frederick, who had warned him of the strong feeling of support in Germany for Luther's work.

In October 1520, Charles went to Aachen to be crowned Emperor. The Elector Frederick was on his way to participate in the coronation but stopped in Cologne to nurse an attack of gout. Here Aleander, the papal nuncio to Germany, asked him to arrest Luther but he refused.

The charges brought against Luther made it clear that the Church considered him beyond the pale. Looked upon first as an errant child, he later became known as a troublemaker and was finally condemned as a heretic. The best minds of the Church were engaged in the conflict but were unsuccessful in challenging Luther's propositions. By the time of the Diet at Worms, the Elector Frederick had fended off threats from Cajetan, Miltitz, Eck, and Aleander. He had, after counsel with Erasmus, Spalatin, Pfeffinger, and a few others, refused to name Luther a heretic without proper hearing by his peers. He agreed that no scriptural evidence had been adduced to confute Martin. When the Elector faced demands to take Luther into custody, he defied both ecclesiastical and civil authority. Frederick was a friend and protector indeed.

Luther knew what was happening. He was aware of the dangers to himself and realized his great debt to the Elector. It was a peculiar relationship in that they never engaged in face-to-face conversation. They probably were in the same room only on one occasion, outside of the appearance before the Diet at Worms when Luther centered his attack on indulgences and the veneration of relics—two practices close to the Elector's heart.

In October 1518, Cardinal Cajetan, the Pope's representative, had written a sharp letter demanding that the Elector surrender Luther to be remanded to the Pope and the Curia: "Examine your conscience and send Brother Martin to Rome or exile him from your country." This last would open Luther to apprehension by other authorities. Frederick not only refused but sent the letter to Luther who passed it on to his faculty colleagues at Wittenberg. They returned it to Martin with the request that the Elector not comply with Cajetan's demand. Regardless of the Elector's distaste for some of the Reformer's writings and public expression, Luther could hardly have had a better friend and a more faithful patron.

Even with all the concerns and activity, Luther remained involved in the day-to-day operations of the University of Wittenberg. He tended to his own teaching schedule and was in regular contact with the Elector, who made most final decisions on such matters as teaching loads, curriculum, enrollment, salaries of professors, appointments of new professors—all of the administrative problems of an on-going, growing institution. In 1520, having acceded to the Elector's appointment of Melanchthon two years earlier, Luther got in touch with Frederick through Spalatin to urge an increase in Philipp's salary.

Through Spalatin, the Elector consulted with the Reformer on a variety of electorate concerns. Among the secular leaders accepting the Lutheran proposals of reform was Ulrich von

Hutten. Shortly before the Diet at Worms, Hutten suggested to the Elector Frederick that he secularize all monastic enterprises in Electoral Saxony, keeping their wealth in Germany rather than seeing it all go to Rome. On such matters as this, as well as the radical early reforms carried out by Hutten and the Knight Franz von Sickingen, Frederick frequently turned to Luther for assessment on a variety of proposals and actions.

Through all this activity, Luther became more and more abrasively critical of the Church and clergy, both in public and privately. On November 28, 1520, the Emperor Charles wrote to the Elector Frederick from Oppenheim, ordering him to bring Luther to Worms to appear before the coming Diet "in order to give him the full hearing before the learned and competent persons." He promised that no harm would come to Luther and instructed the Elector that he require that Luther write nothing against the Pope. But between the coronation of the Emperor in October and his letter telling the Elector to bring Luther to Worms, Aleander, the papal nuncio, encouraged the burning of Luther's works at Louvain, Cologne, and Mainz. The Elector refused to order the burning in his domains and ignored the Papal Bull *Exsurge Domine* completely in spite of Eck's and Aleander's demands that he honor it.

As the year 1520 came to a close, Luther's friends and students, led by Philipp Melanchthon, planned a book-burning of their own. Philipp posted a notice that on December 20 everyone was invited to a bonfire and urged to bring official church writings and doctrinal presentations, with the Papal Bull to be the *piece de resistance*. The Elector is reported to have been notified, and he suggested that papal decretals be added to the fire. On December 20 he had written to Charles V, refusing to require Luther's presence at the Diet set for early in 1521. The Emperor and the Elector agreed that Luther should remain in

Wittenberg until they had a chance to talk personally on the matter.

The Elector suffered some pressure from fellow electors, as well as from Church leaders because of his wariness at handing Luther to the authorities. In this explosive situation, Luther had written to Spalatin when the demand was to send him to Rome: "I now need your help more than ever . . . use your influence with the Sovereign and Pfeffinger (the Elector's counselor) to obtain for me from the Pope the return of my case, so that I can be tried before German judges." Luther gave some thought to refuge in Bohemia, perhaps thinking it appropriate for one accused of being a Hussite. Franz von Sickingen offered protection in his castle. But Aleander was reporting to Rome in the latter part of 1520 that there was restiveness among the German princes as well as bishops; that the Archbishop of Mainz, a good friend of Frederick the Wise, had advisers who were anti-Rome; and that the Elector, while still a loyal Catholic, was being directly influenced by active followers of Brother Martin. The Elector resisted the pressures and provided Luther with a sense of security in continuing his residence in Wittenberg. Frederick's minister, Hans von Planitz, conveyed word of the Elector's support to the council in Wittenberg.

After the Diet at Worms was convened in January 1521 with over two hundred official delegates, including princes, dukes, Landgraves, cardinals and archbishops, plus assorted ambassadors and representatives from various countries, there was much discussion about affairs of the empire. They brought the new young Emperor up-to-date on problems and relationships. The Elector Frederick was the leader of the German contingent, at least on the secular side, and because of his protection of Luther, was looked upon with disfavor by the ecclesiastical leaders. When he was given a copy of the Edict of

"Here I Stand . . ." Luther in appearance at the Diet of Worms, 1521.

Excommunication, he gave it back, saying it was not accurate because it named him as one of those who had led Luther into heresy. He reiterated his profession of innocence of any first-hand knowledge of the Friar's teachings and insisted that his only concern was that Luther's teaching had not been fairly appraised by competent judges. Luther eased the pressure on the Elector by letting him know, through Spalatin, that he was willing to come to Worms if he could have a safe-conduct, and if he was not there just to recant.

Appearing before the Diet on April 17, 1521, Luther was not without friends, chief of whom at this time was undoubtedly the Elector. The Emperor Charles was seated on a raised dais. His brother, Ferdinand, who much later succeeded him on the imperial throne, stood to one side. On the other side were the seven prince-electors, most prominently Frederick the Wise of

Saxony who carried the imperial sword. Before the Emperor were many prelates in full canonicals, plus the Pope's official representatives, Aleander and Caraciolo. Luther stood alone as John Eck asked the two pertinent questions, first in Latin, then in German: Are these your writings? Will you retract the doctrines therein? Luther asked for time to consider his answers, and he was given twenty-four hours to make his reply. The next day Brother Martin's defense before the assembled dignataries was brief and to the point: "Unless I am convinced by the testimony of the Scriptures or by clear reason (for I do not trust either in the Pope or in councils alone, since it is well known that they have often erred and contradicted themselves), I am bound by the Scriptures I have quoted and my conscience is captive to the Word of God. I cannot and I will not retract anything, since it is neither safe nor right to go against conscience. Here I stand. I can do no other. May God help me. Amen." Some worried historians insist that he did not say, "Here I stand . . ." but in his own later recounting of the event, the Reformer affirmed that these were his very words.

The Elector was happy with the beleaguered monk's response and by the way he presented himself before such an intimidating audience. In his later telling of the experience, Luther wrote: "While I was speaking, they demanded I repeat it all in Latin." Though witnesses said he was perspiring heavily, he said, "But I repeated every word in Latin, wherewith my prince Elector, Duke Frederick, was very well pleased." It may be that the Emperor did not press the attack on Luther out of deference to the Elector Frederick with whom negotiations were in process at the time for a marriage between a nephew of the Elector and the Emperor's sister.

Friends of Luther, overjoyed at what he had said, and how he had comported himself before the Diet, gathered at his lodging that evening. Spalatin wrote, "The doctor's little room could not contain all the visitors who presented themselves. I saw among them Duke Wilhelm of Brunswick, Landgrave Philip of Hesse, Count Wilhelm of Hanneberg, the Elector Frederick, and many others." Surprisingly, this was the first time the monk and his prince Elector had ever met face-to-face, and this may have been the only time.

The Diet voted an edict, placing Luther under imperial ban. He was subject to arrest and execution as a heretic. The safe-conduct was sufficient to get him back to Wittenberg, but any friends who might help him or follow him were not protected, being themselves subject to arrest and punishment. The Elector faced a difficult problem: if he aided Luther, even though he was a Prince-Elector, he would also be subject to the edict. In the face of this, how could he protect Luther? The Wittenberg Doctor had pleased him greatly at Worms, and now more than ever he was moved to protect his professor. Faced with this dilemma, Frederick planned to "kidnap" Luther and take him out of circulation. In order to cover his own tracks in the plan, he talked with Spalatin, and perhaps one or two others, but stayed away from carrying out the details so that he could profess innocence if questioned by the authorities.

Shortly before leaving Worms, with the same small group of friends who had come there with him, Luther was told by Spalatin that the Elector was concerned for his safety and that he would be taken to a safe place. Specific details as to where, when and how this was to happen were not given. There is some evidence that Nicholas Amsdorf, a traveling companion and close friend, was "in" on the plot.

The Elector, greatly pleased with Luther's conduct at Worms, provided for him to be set upon by armed horsemen as he traveled to Wittenberg. When told of the "kidnapping," the citizens and University people were convinced that Luther was dead and the imperial edict had been enforced. The Elector felt that keeping Luther at the Wartburg Castle would give time for the storm to blow itself out.

While he was at the Wartburg, Luther kept in touch with Spalatin. This means that he was also in touch with the Elector, who was very disturbed by the events taking place in Wittenberg. There Carlstadt and Zwilling took the lead in instituting a number of reforms. Carlstadt doffed his monk's robes and dressed as a peasant. He married a fifteen-year-old girl. With Zwilling he began serving communion with both wine and bread and advocated the destruction of the statues in the churches. He also wrote against celibacy and otherwise antagonized the citizenry and the Elector, who was less ready than the people for radical change in the life of the Church.

The Elector was a deeply religious, moral man known for his piety and concern for his people. He was upset by the excesses in the reforms undertaken by Carlstadt and Zwilling. It is possible that he was cautious in his approach to such matters as the renunciation of celibacy by monks and nuns because of his own experience. Never having married, he had an early liaison with a young woman, Anna Weller. She was a commoner, which removed her from possibility of marriage. She bore him three children, two sons and a daughter. His love for her remained constant throughout his life. Some suggest that Luther's awareness of this situation may have entered into his defense of the bigamous marriage of Philip of Hesse at a much later date.

At the Wartburg, Luther heard what was happening, and he, too, felt that Carlstadt and Zwilling were moving too fast. He was so disturbed that he made a quick trip to Wittenberg in December 1521 to meet with Justus Jonas, Philipp Melanchthon, Nicholas Amsdorf, and others to discuss the situation.

The Elector, who had expressed his displeasure with the reforms of Carlstadt and Zwilling, not only reproved them, but asked that Melanchthon, Jonas, and Amsdorf assume more control. Luther agreed with the Elector, and in his meeting with his friends urged that they ameliorate the situation. In March 1522, he came to the conclusion that the radical Reformers were still too active, and, over the objections of the Elector, returned to Wittenberg. Frederick wanted him to stay longer in the Wartburg, fearing for his safety should he leave its protective walls.

Luther was concerned that Melanchthon, Jonas, and Amsdorf had been persuaded to join in the more radical reforms, which had also drawn in most of the Augustinian monks. So many of the monks left the Black Cloisters that when Martin Luther and Katherine von Bora were married in 1525, the Elector's successor, John the Steadfast, gave them the monastery as a place to live. While Luther was still at the Wartburg, Philipp Melanchthon admonished Frederick on his "duty" as a Christian prince to take a hand in eliminating the abuses of the Mass in his dominions. Philipp told the Elector that the "salvation of his soul" required any Christian prince to prohibit worship in the Catholic tradition. The patience of Frederick was tried even more by the excesses of Thomas Müntzer, preacher at Allstadt, who wanted to kill off the "godless," by which he meant those who remained orthodox Catholics.

Luther considered the situation to be out of hand. He knew he needed to be back at his post as leader of the Reformation. His security was in God, and he said as much to the Elector when he wrote to him about leaving the Wartburg. He assured his Prince that he "had received the Gospel not from men, but from heaven alone, through our Lord Jesus Christ," and that his real protector was God. He had also written to Spalatin that he wanted to be commended to the Elector, his "most illustrious sovereign," and requested that his departure from the Wartburg and arrival in Wittenberg be kept secret. It was evident that he did not want the Elector to worry about him. In keeping with his doctrine of church and state, he also told the Elector in a letter that "in the sight of men it behooves your Electoral Highness to act as follows. . . ." What followed was an expression of Luther's idea to what extent he might expect the Elector to protect him. "An Elector to render obedience to the power established and allow his Imperial Majesty to dispose of life and property in the lands and towns subject to your Electoral Highness, as is right and in accordance with the laws of the Empire, nor to oppose or resist, or seek to place any obstacle or hindrance in the way of the aforesaid power should it wish to lay hands on me to kill me."

By the time Luther had returned to Wittenberg on March 7, 1522, he had let the Elector know that he was acting against the Elector's wishes, and that he did not ask for protection. "I know that my coming to reside in your Electoral Grace's city is without your Electoral Grace's knowledge or consent." He acknowledged that this endangered Elector Frederick as well as himself, but that there was substantial reason for his return.

The Junker George returned from the Wartburg as Professor Martin Luther because the people of Wittenberg wanted him back. The problems they were experiencing were a result of Luther's teachings and couldn't be handled by correspondence. They feared rebellion by the German people. Luther expressed all of this in a letter to the Elector, intended for presentation to the Saxon princes who were meeting in Nuremberg, so they might present it to the Emperor's representative residing there. Luther sent a draft of this letter to Spalatin, suggesting that he would sign it, including whatever postscript the Elector might add. Spalatin rewrote the letter, and with additions by the Elector, it went to the princes at Nüremberg.

It should be noted that the Elector was not a blind supporter of Luther. He made a distinction between toleration and assent, which was fortunate for Luther, since Frederick was a tolerant man, although he never officially crossed the line to the Reformation faith. He also was a thoughtful man, with compassion for his subjects and an eye for the implications and consequences of his actions, political as well as ecclesiastical. Upon occasion he reminded Luther of his authority as Elector, sometimes by refusing to act, sometimes by postponing or delaying action to a more propitious time. The Elector appointed Melanchthon to the faculty of the University over the objections of Luther, who supported another candidate. When Luther asked for an increase in salary for Philipp at the time of his marriage, the Elector held off for some months. John Bugenhagen came to the faculty, but again the Elector was slow to respond to Luther's request for the new professor to be paid.

In a number of critical situations, the Elector did not agree with either words or actions of the Reformer. Frederick was his own man, not only among the German princes, but among his professors of theology. He had difficulty coming to terms with many of the Reformation ideas. In 1521, the Archbishop of Mainz proposed a sale of indulgences in Halle. Luther, by this time the avowed opponent of all indulgences, wrote a book against this particular sale. The Elector was convinced that the book would disturb the peace and told Spalatin to tell Luther to withhold publication. Luther was angered by this request and berated not only the Archbishop for authorizing the indulgence but also the Elector for daring to order that the book not to be published. Luther wrote to Spalatin: "I will not put up with it. I will rather lose you and the prince himself and every living being. If I have stood up against the Pope, why should I yield to this creature?" However, the book was not published, and the Elector prevailed.

More often Luther made proposals and the Elector acquiesced, either for reasons of state, or because Spalatin pushed, or because the proposal was reasonable and good for the people. Many of the reform ideas proposed by Luther lifted material or spiritual burdens from the people. The Elector was wise enough to recognize this and to support and encourage the Reform Movement, even though he continually protested his total loyalty to the old Church. Frederick was not enthusiastic about the emptying of the monasteries and convents, but when Luther began using the Black Cloisters as a place of refuge for both monks and nuns who were forsaking their vows, he did not make trouble for Luther. Luther had encouraged their defection from the orders and then had come to him for a place for them to stay.

In 1523–1524, all the Augustinians were gone, and the Black Cloister had become a kind of "half-way house." Luther wrote to the Elector that "I am now living in this monastery alone, except for the Prior. The Prior expects to leave soon, and in any case I cannot endure the daily moaning of the people whom I must remind to pay the rents." So the Black Cloister was handed back to the Elector who let Luther keep on living there and said nothing about the way the monastery was used by de-cowled monks and nuns. A couple of years later, the Elector's successor gave the Black Cloister to Luther as a permanent residence.

As Prince-Elector, Frederick shared in many of what could be called administrative details of the budding Reform Movement and had a hand in many of the appointments of evangelical pastors, even though he professed to be no Luther follower himself. At Eilenberg there were a number of the townsfolk who wanted a pastor in the evangelical mold. They believed that if the Elector opened the way their city council could apply for such a pastor. Luther wrote to Spalatin asking him to get a letter from the Elector requesting their councilors to "yield to their own people in this vital and sacred matter." By this circuitous route the councilors sent their request for one of the preachers the Elector proposed, and it was done. At nearby Altenburg, the people resisted the appointment of a Lutheran preacher, but the Elector sent one anyway.

An interesting sidelight on the participation of the Elector in the appointment of evangelical pastors is that Spalatin was involved in all the negotiations. Spalatin followed Luther in all his sympathies, yet his own village church in Spalt remains Catholic to this day. In 1522, Spalatin, noted for his close relationship with the Elector and still officially a good Catholic, gave the local church in Spalt a statue of the Virgin Mary which was duly installed in a niche in the facade of the church where it still may be seen. The burgomaster's office has a very brief historical note about Spalatin: "The most famous citizen of our town was Spalatin, a monk who helped Martin Luther introduce the so-called Reformation (1517). The statue of the Holy Virgin Mary (about 1522) is a present to his fathertown. Thanks to this Spalt never changed its faith and remained Catholic."

In 1524 at the Diet of Nuremberg, Cardinal Campeggio arrived bearing a letter from Pope Clement VII to Frederick the Elector, with expressions of goodwill toward all Germans. The Elector had left the Diet before the Legate's arrival, so Campeggio wrote his own letter to him, noting that he had heard that the Elector "was a favorite of the new heresies." The Pope, said Campeggio, wanted to warn all princes, and most especially Frederick, of the danger to Germany in his actions.

What Campeggio had not sensed was that the Elector Frederick was at his best when resisting just this kind of pressure.

Luther knew well how great a friend he had lost when Frederick died. From time to time he had been openly critical of the Prince. In 1523, he wrote of his Elector, "His way of acting does not please me, for it savours of . . . unbelief and courtly infirmity of soul, preferring temporal to spiritual things." This echoed his tract of 1522 on "Secular Authority; to What Extent it Should Be Obeyed." Here, he said, "You must know that from the very beginning of the world a wise prince was a rare bird indeed; still more a pious prince. They are usually the greatest fools or the worst knaves on earth." One of the Bavarian chancellors called this a "call to revolution." Duke George, one of Luther's persistent enemies, said it was scandalous, and proposed that his cousin, the Elector Frederick, suppress it. Frederick refused such a suggestion; as always he believed the truth would prevail. While the Reformer did not exempt his own Prince from such criticisms, he recognized publicly and privately that Frederick was his "Gracious Sovereign," his benefactor, his defender, and his protector.

After a reign of thirty-nine years, Frederick the Wise died on May 5, 1525. Melanchthon and Luther were not at his bedside, but George Spalatin, his secretary and confidant, was, with what consolation he could offer. As chaplain, Spalatin administered communion with both bread and wine, which the Elector received in at least a symbolic acceptance of Luther's teachings. There was no administration of the last rites in the Catholic tradition.

The Prince had wanted and worked for peace in his realm, but had found little of it. In the struggles of the developing Reformation he had maintained a level of concern for truth and reason that was not always recognized or appreciated. Up to his last hours he was a professing, loyal Roman Catholic, but his frank recognition of its shortcomings and abuses made him an open defender of Martin Luther, the Friar of Wittenberg, who also searched for truth and found it 180 degrees away from his royal support.

Frederick did not defend Luther's proposals so much as his right to express them, so long as they were not refuted by Scripture. He defended Luther even when the monk was defying him and maligning him personally. His faculties remained alert to the end, and to the end he was sorting out values. He was tired and disheartened by his apparent failure to establish peace for his home country, Saxony: "Alas, if it were God's will I should die with joy. I see neither love nor truth, nor any good thing upon earth."

The courage and wisdom and moderation of Frederick did not put a damper on Luther's impetuous, bull-headed, compelling personality—rather, it provided a security in which Luther could do his work. Because he was who he was and where he was, his support put a protective sheltering frame around Luther's Reformation. His peers in the nobility looked up to him; the Emperor listened to him and was guided by him; the Pope in Rome respected him and feared to displease him. Such confidence and respect made it possible for Frederick the Wise to be a friend to Martin Luther and his protector.

The "Luther Denkmal" in Worms is correct in placing Frederick—Friedrich der Weise—out in front, among the great leaders of the Reformation, a little lower than Luther himself but at his right hand.

CHAPTER 10

Katherine von Bora

A good wife who can find?" The question is attributed to Lemuel, King of Massa, in the Old Testament book of Proverbs. It is a question that keeps recurring and was certainly a question of significance for the monks and priests of the sixteenth century in Germany. There Luther was an important agent in the process of putting wife with husband, in one of the more significant changes in Church practice and social acceptance. Along with the radical shifts in acceptance of papal authority, both civil and religious, the understanding of the Mass or Lord's Supper, and the concept of salvation by faith alone, Luther attacked the vow of celibacy by priests, monks, and nuns. By common consensus, this was an action that threatened to undercut the whole forward movement of the Reformation.

Luther moved gradually to the position that monastic and priestly vows were not necessarily binding, along with his growing insistence on scriptural warrant for whatever the Church required by way of belief and practice. The celibate

vows were based on the Roman Catholic position—as opposed
to that of the Greek Catholics—that there is a separation
between clergy and laity. Luther believed that Scripture, beginning with Adam and Eve, recognized the marriage relationship
as normative and God's plan for human life; and the doctrine of
the priesthood of all believers erased any theological warrant
for the monastic vows.

As a youth, Luther seemed to have a clear understanding of
marriage, along with a ready acceptance of the monastic vows as
a requirement of the Church. However, his critique of celibacy
in the treatise "To the Christian Nobility" led to unforeseen
consequences. While hidden away at the Wartburg he heard the
news of priests and monks and nuns marrying. His first reaction was: "Good heavens! Will our Wittenbergers give wives to
monks? They won't give me a wife." But he did sit down and
write "On Monastic Vows," a treatise which he sent to Spalatin.
Spalatin cautiously delayed publication, thinking it to be
entirely too frank.

The treatise repudiated the validity of monastic vows and
made plain Luther's approval of the marriage of priests and
nuns. This did not mean that Luther was ready to think of
marriage as an appropriate estate for himself. He expected
martyrdom for himself in the near future. He thought he would
be put to death as the response of the Church to his teachings
and criticisms. So, although he was happy to see the marriage
of monks and nuns, the idea of marriage for himself was
unthinkable.

Some of Luther's ideas on the marriage relationship border
on the ribald: copulation is sinful, even in marriage, but "God
covers the sin." At one point he is critical of the human method
of procreation, that it was somewhat awkward, mechanically

speaking. He suggested that had God consulted him, "I should have advised him to continue the generations of species by fashioning human beings out of clay, as Adam was made." He made jokes about the business of love-making. In a letter to Spalatin, he refers to himself as a "famous lover," a reference to his having taken care of several nuns at the Black Cloister while completing arrangements for their possible marriage.

His more serious ideas about marriage, and specifically the marriage of nuns, were tied to his thinking about monastic vows. In April 1523, he published a brief tract, "Basis and Rationale for Permitting Young Women to Leave the Convent." He dedicated this to Leonard Koppe, who earlier that month had spirited twelve nuns from the convent at Nimbschen, near Grimma, and left nine of them in Luther's care.

Luther had encouraged nuns to escape from the confines of conventual life and find a new, more open life outside. His public approval led a number of nuns to escape, an adventurous proposition since abducting nuns or otherwise aiding them to leave the convent was a capital offense. Frederick the Wise did not approve of nuns relinquishing their vows but did not exact the penalty when they or their deliverers were apprehended. Duke George, Frederick's brother, was not so gentle, insisting on the death penalty for those caught and found guilty. Many of the liberated nuns found positions as domestics, some married priests or monks, and others married laymen. The sisters sometimes sought the counsel of Luther as they struggled with their new evangelical understandings.

One such group of nuns at Nimbschen discovered the contrast between the life of the cloister and their newfound understanding. Nine of them wrote to their parents, asking for sanctuary as they proposed leaving the convent. "The salvation of our souls," they said, "will not permit us to continue to live longer within the seclusion of the cloister." The families of the young women, frightened by the consequences they might face, refused their daughters' pleas. Luther is thought to have made the arrangements for them to be taken from the convent by two respected burghers of Torgau, although he said afterwards, "It is not I who have done this, but would to God that I could thus emancipate every captive conscience, and empty every convent in the world; the breach in their walls is made." On April 7, 1523, Leonard Koppe and Wolff Tolmitzsch picked up the twelve nuns in a covered wagon, disguising them as a load of herring. They eventually arrived at the Black Cloister in Wittenberg, where Luther began finding places for them. Three returned to their own homes. A student is reported to have said, "A wagon load of vestal virgins has just come to town, all more eager for marriage than for life. God grant them husbands lest worse befall."

Although he had no resources and the cloister was a poor place to harbor them, Luther undertook to restructure their lives. He wrote to his friend Spalatin: "Grace and peace. Nine fugitive nuns, a wretched crowd, have been brought to me by honest citizens of Torgau . . . there is no cause for suspicion . . . You ask what I shall do with them? First I shall inform their relatives and ask them to support the girls; if they will not, I shall have the girls otherwise provided for. Some of the families have already promised me to take them; for some I shall get a husband if I can. Their names are Magdalene von Staupitz (the sister of John von Staupitz), Elsa von Conitz, Ave Gross, Margaret and Catherine Zeschau, and Katherine von Bora." Then Luther went on to ask Spalatin to raise some money to help the cause. The last thing Luther had in mind was that he could possibly be one of those to marry one of the nuns.

When Luther met Katherine von Bora, his thinking on the marriage of priests and nuns had evolved from early acceptance of the concept of celibacy and the monastic vows of chastity, to growing doubts about the vows themselves, to a desire to reconcile the current of increasing "immorality" among the clergy with his understanding of Scripture, to a growing sense that change was in the air and that the change should be encouraged.

Katherine von Bora was born in January 1499 of a poor but noble family on the Lippendorf estate south of Leipzig. At the tender age of five, after the death of her mother, her father, having remarried, placed her in a convent school. At sixteen she took the veil as a Cistercian nun. Two aunts were in the same convent. Portraits of Katie may or may not do her justice. One older text says that she was "not remarkable for beauty." A later writer says that, while of good birth and character, she was "hardly designed to arouse precipitous passion."

While working in the home of the burgomaster of Wittenberg, after escaping from the nunnery, Katherine fell in love with a patrician student at the University, Jerome Baumgartner. When he returned to his Nuremberg home, his family objected to the proposed marriage, and Jerome rejected her. She learned of his rejection through Luther but refused the suggestion that she marry a Dr. Glatz, saying she would marry only Dr. Amsdorf or Luther himself. It may be that she was trying to talk herself out of the idea of marriage, since Amsdorf and Luther, both forty-two, were thought to be beyond the normal age at which men married.

But Luther surprised all his friends by announcing his intent to marry Katherine von Bora. One factor in his decision was he felt that he ought to marry and have children in order to satisfy his parents' desire that there be another generation to carry on the Luther name. In addition, Martin had for a long time felt that he owed his father some payback for his having left the study of the law for the less-rewarding—to his father—study of theology. The Luthers were overjoyed at the word of the coming nuptials and their special invitation to be present at the wedding celebration.

Although Martin did not count it among the important reasons why he should marry, he gave serious consideration to the effect his marriage would have on the Reformation Movement. Thinking he could conceivably be burned at the stake within a year, he did not anticipate starting a family, but by marrying Kate he wanted to give legitimacy to his public position against celibacy. When Albert, the Archbishop of Mainz—one of Luther's most persistent enemies—was giving consideration to following the example of his cousin, Albert of Brandenburg, in secularizing his domain, Martin wrote to a friend: "If my marrying will strengthen him, I am ready. I believe in marriage, and I intend to get married before I die, even though it should only be a betrothal like Joseph's." As it turned out, Albert did not secularize his bishopric but continued his opposition to the reform proposals and leadership.

Luther's stated reasons for getting married were to please his father, to spite the Pope and the devil, and to establish his personal witness before being burned at the stake. He did not say that he loved Katherine, even though he said in May 1525 that he would marry her before he died. Since he anticipated imminent death, this could only have been a means to give status to Kate. One wonders what she may have been thinking when he told his friends, "I am not infatuated." Fortunately, he added, " . . . though I cherish my wife." Interestingly, all that we know about their courtship and subsequent marriage is from the letters of Luther and his friends, with nothing from Katie.

Although later on she was an avid correspondent, at least with her husband, we have nothing that tells us what she thought of the looks or the possibilities in the Reformer—only her word that she would have Amsdorf or Luther, or none. And the record seems clear that she accepted Martin on the rebound, having been rejected by Baumgartner.

Luther gave advice and counsel concerning marriage to his friends and to any who asked. Wolfgang Reissenbusch, preceptor in the monastery of St. Anthony, in Lichtenberg, Saxony, had talked with Luther about the vows of celibacy and his desire to marry a young woman in Torgau. In March 1525, two and a half months before his own marriage, Luther wrote: "I have often been spoken to about matrimony and have observed that you are not only suited for and inclined toward marriage, but are also forced and compelled by God himself, who created you therefor. . . . We are all made for marriage, as our bodies know and as the Scripture states: 'It is not good that man should be alone; I will make a helpmate for him' . . . it is said that it takes a bold man to venture to take a wife. What you need above all else, then, is to be encouraged, admonished, urged, incited, and made bold . . . Stop thinking about it and go to it right merrily. Your body demands it. God wills it and drives you to it . . . " On April 26, just a month after receiving this counsel, Reissenbusch was married to one Anne Herzog in Torgau. Even as he wrote, Martin was probably thinking also of his own situation, for he married Katherine von Bora just two months later.

Having made up his mind that he would marry Katherine, Luther wasted no time in accomplishing the deed. About this time Spalatin, who was himself thinking of marriage, asked Luther his thoughts on long engagements. His friend replied on June 10, "Don't put off till tomorrow! By delay Hannibal lost Rome. By delay Esau forfeited his birthright. Christ said, 'Ye

Painting of Luther by his friend Cranach.

shall seek me, and ye shall not find.' Thus Scripture, experience, and all creation testify that the gifts of God must be taken on the wing." Three days later, on June 13, Luther and Katie were married before a group of friends and family in the Black Cloister. Pastor John Bugenhagen officiated at the ceremony, with Lucas Cranach and his wife, Justus Jonas, and John Apel, professor of law at the University of Wittenberg as witnesses. Following the custom of the time, a celebration, sometimes called the wedding, was held two weeks later on June 27, again at the Black Cloister which the new Elector John the Steadfast gave to the Luthers for a home. By this time the Augustinian monks had all left the Order and the monastery. For some unexplained reason, Philipp Melanchthon, widely considered to be one of Luther's closest friends, was not invited to the marriage, although he was one of the guests at the wedding celebration.

Martin's parents were at the marriage ceremony as were the Cranachs, (for a wedding gift, Lucas Cranach painted their portraits). George Spalatin was there and Leonard Kopp, the rescuer of the nuns, who brought a barrel of Torgau beer. Nicholas Amsdorf was also present. The University gave the new couple a silver goblet, a barrel of Embech beer, and money, both in silver and gold coin. Albert, the Archbishop of Mainz, with whom Luther had tangled on many occasions and who resisted the Reformation to the end, sent twenty gold gulden. Martin refused this gift, but the prudent Katie kept it.

Luther was a man of his time; he did not marry in order to have a colleague in his work; rather he believed that the vows of celibacy were not in God's plan and that marriage was a natural estate. As a man of his times he believed that women have their own area of concerns and responsibilities and should not get mixed up with a man's. The man is the head of the house and she the wife. He should rule her with gentleness, but

Martin Luther.   *Katherine von Bora.*

he should rule. Once Luther said that women are created with large hips, and they should stay home and sit on them! Children, like the wife, are to be totally ruled by the father and husband. Children who show disrespect for their parents are breaking the Ten Commandments, a concept that Luther upheld when he once refused for three days to forgive his son for some minor dereliction. The offense was not grave, and Katie had others intercede on behalf of the boy, who had begged his father's pardon. But Luther was adamant for three whole days. He conveniently forgot how he had disobeyed his own father to become a monk. At the dinner following his ordination his father reminded him that the Ten Commandments were still in force, even for monks.

After some time, Luther's view of marriage began to change and more and more his wife became his partner in every venture. Her eventual full participation in his life began with her pressure to keep him from going to the wedding of his dear friend, Spalatin, in November 1525. He wrote a letter of apology for not being present, referring to the danger he was in when he traveled from his home: "This is the reason why I cannot visit you, for I am constrained by the tears of my wife, Katie, who believes as you write, that you desire nothing else than to put me in danger." Amsdorf had called her attention to the possible danger in travel, and so, "The argument that she uses is that I have a high regard for Amsdorf's opinion." This was not the last time that Katie gave substance to his frequent name for her: "My Lord Katie." Very shortly Katie took over the running of the Luther household.

She brought no dowry to the marriage, and Martin had little or nothing. Fortunately, the Elector gave them a place to live in addition to doubling Luther's teaching salary. Upon many occasions the Prince sent them game and sometimes wine and clothing as well. Luther was no manager, though, often giving away just about everything they had. His generosity so often outran his resources that Cranach, who was his banker as well as artist friend, refused to honor his checks. Martin was light-hearted about such mundane matters, once saying, "I do not worry about debts, because as Katie pays one, another one comes." He wrote to a friend that he was sending a vase as a wedding present, but had to add a postscript, "Katie's hid it."

The reaction of Luther's friends to his marriage was varied. Some thought he had done damage to the evangelical movement. Others thought he had given the gossipmongers too much ammunition. The Catholic authorities were, of course, scandalized. Luther's friends, after their initial shock, to a man defended his right to marry and his reasons for doing so. Melanchthon, who was not invited to the June 13 ceremony, at first had some questions but quickly got beyond them. He wrote two letters to a friend, Joachim Camerarius, which announced the wedding. In the first he wrote, "You might be amazed at this unfortunate time (the Peasants' War), when good and excellent men everywhere are in distress, he not only does not sympathize with them, but, as it seems, rather was wanton and diminishes his reputation." Then he continues, "When I see Luther in low spirits and disturbed by his change of life, I make my best efforts to console him kindly, and since he has done nothing that seems to me worthy of censure or incapable of defense. Besides this, I have unmistakable evidence of his godliness, so that for me to condemn him is impossible."

After his initial shock, Melanchthon wrote to Wenceslaus Link, urging him to come to the June 27 wedding celebration. In his letter he prayed "for good fortune and blessings" on the Reformer in his marriage and new life. The University community was happy with the whole enterprise and took the day off to celebrate.

Justus Jonas, who was present at the June 13 wedding party, reported the next day to Spalatin: "Seeing that night I had to give way to my feelings and could not refrain from tears. Now that it has happened and is the will of God, I wish this good and true man and beloved father in the Lord much happiness." This was the consensus of Luther's friends, and the marriage became an example for family life among pastors from that time on.

It should be noted that in the Luther household Katie set the table, provided substantially for the food that was served, joined the Table Talk, and made arrangements to care for the guests constantly invited by Martin to be present. Over the years the Luthers had a garden, which Martin tended, providing a variety of vegetables for the table: melons, cucumbers, beans, peas, cabbage, lettuce. Outside the village was Katie's orchard, yielding apples, pears, grapes, peaches, and nuts. There was a pond, evidently of some size, for it provided carp, pike, and perch. Katie also took care of the barnyard with its hens, ducks, pigs and cows. She brewed the beer Martin drank and took care of the problems resulting from his prodigal generosity. Some years after their marriage, the Luthers bought from Katie's relatives the farm at Zuladorf which had been one of her father's two pieces of property. The farm was at some distance from Wittenberg, so she spent several weeks there each year taking care of the grounds and orchards.

How she was able to oversee everything in this household is difficult to understand. Once Martin remarked that he had an income of two hundred gulden a year, with expenses of five hundred gulden. By economies here and there, along with gifts from the Elector and other appreciative friends, Katie managed. But her responsibilities were great. The household included Martin and Kate, their five children, a hired man, for a time the two daughters and four sons of one of Martin's sisters, Hans Polner, the son of another sister, Anna Strauss, a great-niece, three other children of Martin's relatives, a nephew and niece of the von Bora family, two aunts who helped in the household, and student boarders. To these were added the frequent guests who came for a meal or overnight. You have to wonder how Kate could find either the time or the money for all of this. In one of his letters from his travels Martin asked that she buy some things for the children, since he could not find suitable gifts at the local fairs and didn't want to come home without something for them.

Luther did not charge lecture fees from students, one of the accepted sources of cash income for University professors. His Wittenberg printer, Hans Lufft, offered him four hundred gulden a year for his works, an offer which Martin refused, saying he was not in the business of writing for money. He

The Black Cloister, home of Martin Luther and Katherine von Bora.

refused Melanchthon's offer of a thousand gulden for his translation of Aesop. The Elector offered him shares in a silver mine worth three hundred gulden a year, upon his completion of his translation of the Bible, but he refused. His work was God's work, and God would take care of him, though Katie must have wondered sometimes how to make ends meet. The family eventually occupied all three stories of the Black Cloister.

In early 1530, Martin urged his aging parents also to come and live with him at the Black Cloister or in a cottage he would provide. Martin wrote: "It would be the greatest joy to me if it were possible for you and mother to come hither, which my Katie and all of us beg you with tears that you will do. . . . My Katie, little Hans, Magdalene, Aunt Lena, and all my household send greetings." His father and mother were in frail health and in need of care but refused, at least for the time. In May 1530, his father died. On May 20, 1531, Luther wrote to his mother when he heard from his brother, James, that she was dying, ending his letter, "All my children and my Katie pray for you. Some weep. Others say before they eat, 'Grandmother is very sick.'"

It is clear that Luther was generous to a fault but that the burden fell upon Kate to make the generosity work. Throughout their married life, Kate helped to hold the evangelical community together with her sympathetic concern for its members. She not only cared for household and family, but for the last and least in Wittenberg. She shared in Martin's generous impulses, although she sometimes held back until she could figure out a way to accommodate them. During the plague of 1527, the entire University moved to the city of Jena, but Martin and Kate stayed in Wittenberg to care for the town's citizens, even at peril to themselves. Both of them had bouts of fever but kept up their caring visits to the sick and dying. Again, in the plague of 1539, when Dr. Seebald Muensterer's family came down with fatal illness, Kate took him and his four children into her home. When Muensterer and his wife both died of the plague, Katherine made a place in the Black Cloister for the continuing care of the children.

Katherine served as both doctor and nurse to Martin through all his illnesses, aches, and pains. She ministered to him when he was at home, and worried about him when he was away. A catalog of his ailments through the years shows that he suffered from dizziness, rheumatism with fever, gout, sciatica, insomnia, constipation, ear inflammations, gallstones, kidney stones, indigestion, hemorrhoids, respiratory problems, and sheer exhaustion. Kate became quite an expert in herbs, massage, and various poultices. She was also well-versed in the folk remedies of the day. Years later, when their son Paul became a doctor and was appointed professor of medicine at the University of Jena, he said, "My mother has helped me and healed many." He said that she was a half doctor herself and that he had learned much from her. It is to a large degree the care that Kate gave Martin that made it possible for him to do the immense work which he did: lecturing, studying, writing, traveling, organizing, and managing the Reformation. Katherine kept him going.

It is important to note that Luther realized her great value to him and her great love for him. Many of Luther's letters are those he wrote to his "Lord Katie." While the marriage may not have had its beginnings in outward expressions of love and affection, these soon came and were reciprocated. Katie shared his Reformation understandings, and he happily joined in her concerns about their children and home. This does not mean that there were not occasional frictions between them. Kate had many reservations about Martin's prodigality and sometimes expressed them. She had no use for Jerome Schurff, a lawyer who was one of the earliest and most devoted followers of Luther. Though Schurff was faithful throughout his life, he didn't always agree with Luther, as in the burning of the Papal Bull. He wrote an unfortunate treatise on the marriage of monks with nuns, which may have been what stirred Katherine's ire. In any case, she would not have him in her house, and the Elector Frederick felt that Martin should try and calm her feelings. It may be that she had heard of Schurff's letter to a friend in which he said, upon hearing that Martin and Katie were to be married, "Should this monk marry, the whole world and the devil himself will laugh, and Luther himself will destroy all he had been building up."

When Katherine wanted something from Martin, or something he might be able to provide through his many contacts, she was not hesitant to ask. In November 1539, Luther wrote to Anthony Lauterbach about a problem in serving communion to the sick. Lauterbach had recently entered a pastorate in Pirna, where he was also the superintendent (or bishop). The custom there was that the pastor should receive Holy Communion each time he served the elements to a sick person, which meant that he might himself communicate several times a day. Luther's recommendation was that he follow the tradition as it had developed but to tell the people in sermons only to receive communion three or four times a year, regularly. This would eliminate the requests for "emergency" services of Communion for those who did not give regular support and attendance to the Church but who expected the Church to be of service to them at any time of need. It would also take away any need to partake of communion himself multiple times a day. After giving advice on this theological matter in the letter to Lauterbach Luther made a request for his wife: "Katie wants the carved door to be as wide as the enclosed measure. The craftsmen will themselves know what length or height to make it. She does not need one of the other doors. Do the best you can to take care of this matter."

Luther's family life was of the utmost importance to him and had a profound effect on his everyday relations with his friends and colleagues. One of the first influences of his marriage was probably on his personal life. He ate better and more regularly, changing from a rather gaunt figure to the more portly, full-cheeked individual we see in later portraits. His personal hygiene also must have improved; he writes, "Before I was married, the bed was not made for a year, but I worked so hard and was so weary that I tumbled in without noticing it." No doubt Katie noticed it and made changes, the changes one would expect after he began waking up and finding, surprisingly, "pigtails on the pillow" beside him.

Martin Luther's happy relationship with Katie and their children reinforced his feelings about the sacredness of family life. This was reflected in his dealings with friends and their families, as well as in the many instances in which he was called upon for advice and counseling in family matters.

Luther was almost forty-three when his first child was born, and he was fifty-two when the last child was born. He was sometimes pretty cranky in dealing with the children. He became a stern disciplinarian and proposed a disciplined approach to child-rearing by his followers. Nevertheless, he was a loving and generous father, devastated when Elizabeth, their second child, died in infancy. He wrote to his friend, Nicholas Hausmann, "My little daughter Elizabeth is dead. It is marvelous how sick at heart . . . it has left me, how much I am moved by grief for her. I would never have believed that a father's heart could become so tender for his children."

When Magdalene died at fourteen, Hans, then sixteen and in school at Torgau, became homesick at the news of his sister's death. Martin wrote to his son three months later. The letter is a combination of consolation at his son's sense of loss and a reminder of how he ought to deal with such tragedy: "Dear Son Hans [John]: Your mother and all the household are well. See to it that you conquer your tears manfully lest you add to your mother's distress and concern. Be obedient to God, who, through us, commands you to work where you now are. Thus you will easily overcome your weakness. Your mother was unable to write, nor did she think it necessary. She wishes to explain that what she told you before (that you may come home if things do not go well with you) was intended to apply in case of illness. Should you become ill, let us know at once. Otherwise she hopes you will stop your lamentations and go on cheerfully and quietly with your studies."

As a composer Luther is best known for the hymn "Ein feste Burg ist unser Gott" (A Mighty Fortress Is Our God), but he also wrote a lovely Christmas hymn for children, sung at the family

Christmas celebration a year after the birth of little Margaret. It is a touching blend of Reformation theology with the life of a closely knit family: "From heaven on high to earth I come to you/and I am bringing you good news,/so very much good news I bring,/It makes me want to shout and sing. . . . What the globe could not unwrap/nestled lies in Mary's lap./Just a baby, very wee,/Yet Lord of all the world is he."

In all this, Katie was a primary influence, shaping the mature Luther into what he presented to the world. She did it by love and affection, combined with an innate ability to deal effectively with life. The Luthers lived in what one writer calls a "glass house," and Katie made it a model presentable to the world. Martin occasionally made what he thought of as humorous remarks about his wife, but these were received in equally good humor and were in reality a mark of his respect for her. He recognized her virtues as a wife and mother and manager. One year he proposed that she improve her first-rate mind by studying Scripture, offering her a fifty gulden reward if she read through the Bible by Easter. In a letter to Justus Jonas, instead of the usual greetings from Kate, he tells a story of her familiar routine in caring for the farms, grazing the cattle she had bought, brewing his beer, with all the travel these tasks entailed—and that he had promised her the reward if she completed her Bible reading in time. Jonas was a dear friend and probably accepted Luther's concerns about Katie's intellectual pursuits, while feeling sorry for Katie!

Much has been made of Luther's Table Talk, and some credit should go to Katie for its significance in understanding of the developing Reformation. She was the one who made it possible by providing the table. Luther, of course, was the drawing card and chief protagonist. After all, it was the Table Talk of Martin Luther. But it was Katie who set the table, made provision for twenty or more to sit down and talk about the Word of God and the ways of God's people. And Katie also joined in the conversation. Melanchthon would dissent upon occasion, but Martin was not often contradicted. Bugenhagen, Melanchthon, and Jonas were frequently at table, and their words helped to keep up Luther's spirits when things were not going well, as did "a word from my Katie." Once when Martin was engaged in an intense discussion with students, his wife broke in with, "Doctor, why don't you stop talking and eat?" Perhaps it was in response to this that Luther once exclaimed, "I wish that women would repeat the Lord's Prayer before opening their mouths." Katherine was kept busy running back and forth from the kitchen, but Luther's comment was: "All my life is patience. I have to have patience with the Pope, the heretics, my family, and Katie."

Wife Katherine resented the fact that some of the friends around the table would record the conversations and later publish them as Table Talk for good profit. Luther refused all offers to realize income from his publications, but some of those who sat around the table had no such compunctions. Veit Dietrich, Conrad Cordatus, Anthony Lauterbach, Heydenreich, John Aurifaber, and others apparently received substantial rewards for their written records of what the great man said. Katie was put out because she thought Martin should have the money from the booksellers and printers. After all, she was the one who had the problem of feeding these friends, colleagues, and in some cases, wives and families. No wonder she sometimes gave a spirited response to her husband's generosity. Her tolerance of his coarseness and prodigality must have worn thin at his refusal to at least accept some of the material benefit which others reaped from his words.

The Table Talk, as published, has some 6,595 entries. Luther comments on just about everything under the sun. Various editors prepared their works after his death, using excerpts from different sources, including some that had already seen print. Katie even thought the students who from time to time joined in the Table Talk should have been charged a "tuition" fee, just as they normally paid for lectures. Someone would ask a question, or respond to a comment by Luther, and the Table Talk was the result. No effort was made to classify one comment as of more import than another, although it is likely that Luther from time to time was probably prescient enough to say, "Listen carefully; this is important."

The Table Talk brought together heavy theological concepts with very down-to-earth expression. From time to time Kate objected to coarseness of language. Martin responded that it was understandable. The range was remarkable:

- God uses lust to impel man to marriage, ambition to office, avarice to earning, and fear to faith.

- Printing is God's latest and best work to spread true religion throughout the world.

- Germany is the Pope's pig. That is why we have to give him so much bacon and sausages.

- A Christian officer in the war with the Turks told his men that if they died in battle they would sup with Christ in paradise. The officer fled. When asked why he did not sup with Christ, he said he was fasting that day.

- "I am the son of a peasant," said Luther, "and the grandson and great-grandson. My father wanted to make me into a burgomaster. Then I became a monk and put off the brown beret. My father didn't like it, and then I got into the Pope's hair and married an apostate nun. Who could have read that in the stars?"

- A melancholic claimed to be a rooster and strutted about crowing. The doctor said that he, too, was a rooster and for several days crowed with him. Then the doctor said, "I am not a rooster anymore, and you are changed, too." It worked.

After being a participant in such Table Talk, it is not surprising that an obviously intelligent Katie would have felt qualified to make suggestions to her husband from time to time in his discourse and correspondence. In 1524, before they were married, Erasmus had published "De Libero Arbitrio," a diatribe against Luther in their controversy on free will. Erasmus's work had reached Wittenberg in September 1524. Luther had only contempt for it. He wrote to Spalatin after a month or so, saying that it had completely disgusted him and that he had been able to read only about eight pages of it. After his marriage to Katherine von Bora the next summer, the controversy heated up again, and she pushed him to reply to the "Diatribe." That he should yield to her urgings in a matter of this kind makes a good case for his growing regard for her intellectual abilities.

Basically, of course, Luther was a child of his own time. Wives had a certain part to play, to be sure, and he expected Katie to play her part. There is much evidence, though, in his letters to her and to others referring to her that he moved far beyond the contemporary understanding of the marriage relationship. Her concerns were relayed in much of his correspondence, especially her personal feelings when she knew of illness or tragedy. When Katherine, the wife of Justus Jonas, died in 1542, the news came as a shock to the Reformer, for there was a very intimate relationship between the Luther family and the Jonas family. The death was presumably a result of complications of childbirth. Martin wrote to his friend, Justus, "My Katie was beside herself (when she heard the news) for she and your wife were intimately united as if they were one soul."

The designation "My Katie" occurs over and over in Luther's correspondence. To Mrs. John Cellarius, whose husband, a professor of Hebrew before he became an Evangelical pastor, died on the eve of being made superintendent (bishop) in Dresden: "I commend you to his [God's] grace. My Katie implores that God's comfort and grace may be yours." When Frederick Myconius, pastor at Zwickau and Gotha lay ill in 1541, Luther wrote to him, adding: "My Katie and all the others, who are deeply moved by your illness, send their greetings." John von Taubenheim was chamberlain in Prussia when his wife died. Luther sent a long letter of consolation to this man who was a tax collector, concluding with, "My Katie sends cordial greetings, bitterly laments your misfortune, and says that if God did not love you so much or if you were a papist, he would not allow you to suffer such a loss. 'He torments his own here, but spares them in the world to come,' as Saint Peter says." In 1534, Luther wrote to Caspar Mueller, chancellor of Mansfeld, a good friend who served as sponsor at the baptism of Luther's oldest child, Hans. Mueller was sick, and Luther wrote a letter of comfort, including a word from his wife, "Have I not visited the sick long enough now? My Lord Katie greets you and hopes that you will be well and will visit us." Conrad Cordatus, one of the Table Talk companions, was bereaved at the death of his infant son in 1530, and Luther expressed not only his own feelings, but "My Katie and our whole household send you greetings."

It was not at all unusual for Luther to refer to Katie as "My Lord Katie" in correspondence and in conversation with others. There is not much question that he was quite aware of how much she came to mean to him as wife, lover, confidante and manager. She was indeed his "Lord" in a kind of feudal sense, for he depended on her gracious resourcefulness to make it possible for him to be what he was.

Luther's awareness of Katherine's resourcefulness was a constantly growing one, expressed frequently in his letters to her, as well as in comments to his close friends. He learned from her and did not hesitate to acknowledge it. A number of times he suggested that she was, in reality, more intelligent and more capable than he. It is hard to know how he could have done all that he did through the years without her.

And in all this, as we have noted, Katie was living with Martin in a glass house. Their wedding was an abomination to the Roman Catholics, under criticism from the beginning, constantly under scrutiny by friends and enemies alike. Luther's followers looked upon the Black Cloister household as a model for the world; his opponents, especially the Romanists, looked upon it as a work of the devil. Though strong on discipline, relationships between parents and children shone through with love and affection, becoming a model that became the standard for pastors' families in the years that followed.

One side note should be added about the importance of Katie in the Luther family life: in October 1541, Luther wrote to Jerome Baumgartner, in Nuremberg, asking a favor. Baumgartner, who as a young man reneged on his proposed marriage with the runaway nun, Katherine von Bora, had become a leader of the Reformation Movement in Nuremberg. Luther wrote to ask that

Baumgartner find a place in a foundling home in Nuremberg for a boy who had been deserted by an Englishman and who had spent a night or two at the Black Cloister in Wittenberg. Martin concluded his letter with this: "She who was once your flame, and who now bears you a new love on account of your admirable virtues and wishes you well with all her heart, respectfully greets you. . . ." Quite obviously Martin and Katherine also had an enviable maturity of relationship.

When they were both older, especially Martin, he frequently expressed to her his concerns that the Reformation had not had much effect on public morality. "God's word is still ignored." While he took much satisfaction in the fact that she, as well as Jonas, Bugenhagen, and Melanchthon were loyal and doing effective work, he was worried that the women wore "shorter skirts behind and lower blouses in front," that public drunkenness had not been diminished, along with other evidence of immorality. His spirits were so low, in fact, that in 1544, on a trip for a wedding in Merseburg, he stopped at Zeitz to visit Amsdorf and wrote to Kate, "I would like to arrange things so that I don't have to return to Wittenberg. My heart has grown cold, and I don't like it there anymore. I also wish you would sell your garden and land, house and all, and I would give the big house back to His Grace. . . . I am tired of the town and I don't want to come back, God willing."

Katherine passed the letter on to the University, where the faculty thought the situation very grave. Melanchthon thought that Luther was troubled, not by the behavior of the people, but by disagreements with Wittenberg city and University officials, and that the decision had come to him on the road. It was not to be taken lightly, as Luther had been talking this way for some time. Melanchthon was delegated to talk with Saxony Chancellor Brück. The Chancellor wrote to the Elector John Frederick, intimating that if Martin remained hardheaded in this, that Philipp Melanchthon would not stay either. John Frederick asked Matthew Ratzeberger, his physician, who was on good terms with Luther, to take a letter to him by way of Wittenberg, seeking counsel of Melanchthon, "since Master Philipppus knows the doctor better than others, and understands his disposition and ways." Matthew was to let Melanchthon read the Elector's letter. Katherine was correct in her feeling that the faculty and the authorities would do all in their power to see that Luther returned to Wittenberg.

Count Albert of Mansfeld, Luther's "beloved Count," was a longtime follower of Martin and one of the first civil authorities to establish the Reformation in a German domain. In 1545, he asked Luther to come to Mansfeld to act as mediator in a dispute with his brother, Count Gebhardt. In October, Martin made the journey to Mansfeld and was unsuccessful in his efforts at mediation. He returned again in December. Matters were still not settled, and Luther made his plans to go again to Mansfeld in January 1546. On January 25, he set out during the worst of the winter, accompanied by his three sons, Hans, Martin, and Paul, as well as a friend, John Aurifaber. Justus Jonas joined the party at Halle. Luther's sons stayed with relatives at Mansfeld while negotiations with the Counts and their lawyers were carried on at Eisleben, Luther's birthplace. After several days an agreement was reached and documents were signed. The boys came to Eisleben from Mansfeld and together with their father made plans for the eighty-mile trip home.

Martin had written almost every day to Katie, and she to him. He rebuked her for her worry, as always in theological terms: "To my dear wife Katherine Luther, doctor's spouse in Wittenberg, keeper of the pig market, and gracious wife whom I am bound to serve hand and foot: grace and peace in the lord. Dear Katie: You should read the Gospel according to Saint John and the Small Catechism, of which you once said, 'Everything in this book has to do with me.' You are worrying in God's stead as if he were not almighty. . . . In order that you may not worry about it, you should know that all the letters which you have written have arrived here. The one you wrote last Friday reached me today along with Master Philipp's letters." Martin wrote again, "To the pious and anxious lady, Mrs. Katherine Luther, of Wittenberg, keeper of Zulsdorf, my gracious and dear wife." He said that the negotiations did not distress them greatly, but they had taken their toll on his frail health.

In all these letters Luther had written to Katie from Eisleben, but he didn't tell her that he was seriously ill. He had written to Melanchthon that he was feeling sick and wished he could escape from the Mansfelders' problems. He said he was "playing the role of a sick goat," ending with "Pray for me that the Lord may bring me back before I am killed by these battles of the wills." February 6 he wrote to Katie and to Melanchthon, asking Philipp to suggest that the Elector send him a letter ordering him home, a move to try to shock the Counts into some harmonious settlement. Luther's sickness grew worse, becoming very serious by February 15.

Michael Coelius, pastor at Mansfeld and chaplain to Count Albert, came to sit at Luther's bedside, joining Jonas and Aurifaber. Tightness in his chest made the Reformer's breathing painful. Some relief was gained through hot towels and brandy, but he was not able to sleep. The Elector's physician was called in but was ineffective, with the pain constantly increasing. At about two in the morning of February 18 he called in his friends. One of the Countesses of Mansfeld was also in the room. Justus Jonas asked him if he continued to hold firm to his reformed doctrines and his answer was a strong "yes." Then Martin called upon them all to pray for him and for "the Lord God and his

Evangelic Church." Scripture came to his lips, as he repeated three times the words of John 3:16 in Latin. Then his sons heard him say, "Father, into Thy hands I commend my spirit." It is thought that his death came as a result of a series of heart attacks.

The slow journey back to Wittenberg drew large crowds of mourners, many of whom followed the procession into town with the body. The Counts of Mansfeld, the Elector of Saxony and his court, all were in attendance at the funeral services as were Martin's brother James and other Mansfeld relatives. But Katherine and the children took precedence over all the other mourners.

In his will, Luther left everything to Katie his Lord, an inheritance that did not provide enough to sustain her household with his salary gone. She had to resist strongly to keep the Elector, whose intentions were of the best, from taking her sons from her in order to give them proper education and care. Luther's words in his will have much to say about how much his wife meant to him: "To my Katherine, because she has always been a gentle, pious and faithful wife to me, has loved me tenderly and has by the blessing of God, given me and brought up for me, five children still living, besides others now dead . . . and more especially because I would not have her dependent on her children, but rather that her children should be dependent on her, honoring and submissive to her. . . ."

For Martin Luther, Paul's letter to the Romans was crucial to his theological understanding. It was Paul's letter to the Romans that inspired Luther's concept of justification by faith. When he insisted on "sole fide"—"by faith alone"—Romans was his reference point. It is therefore a significant measure of his relationship with Katherine as wife, mother, homemaker, and confidant that Luther referred to the Letter to the Romans as, "This is my Katherine von Bora."

Luther Chronology

1483	Martin Luther born, Eisleben, 10 November
1484	Luther family to Mansfeld;
	Huldrich Zwingli born, Wildhaus, Switzerland;
1492	Columbus discovers America
1487–1525	Frederick the Wise, Elector of Saxony
1497–1498	Martin Luther at school at Magdeburg
1498–1501	In Latin School at Eisenach
1501–1505	Student, University of Erfurt
1502	Bachelor of Arts
1505	Master of Arts
1502	Elector Frederick founds University of Wittenberg
1503–1520	John von Staupitz Dean of the theological faculty at Wittenberg
1504	Tetzel sells indulgences in Germany
1505	Luther to Augustinian Monastery, Erfurt (Staupitz)
1507	Luther ordained
1508	Luther teaches at Wittenberg
1509	Called to teach at Erfurt
1509	Henry VIII, King of England;
	John Calvin born
1510	Journey to Rome for Augustinians
1511	Return to Erfurt, transfer to Wittenberg
1512	Doctoral degree conferred;
	Lectures on Genesis
1513	Luther begins lectures on Psalms;
1513	Pope Leo X to Vatican
1515	Luther lectures on Romans
1516	Luther lectures on Galatians;
	Erasmus publishes Greek New Testament;
	Thomas More publishes "Utopia"
1517	31 October, Ninety-five Theses on Castle Church door
1518	26 April, Heidelberg Disputation;
	7 August, Pope Leo cites Luther to Rome;
	8 August, Luther appeals to Elector Frederick;
	25 August, Phillip Melanchthon to Wittenberg to teach;
	12–14 October, Before Cajetan, Augsburg
1519	4–6 January, Luther questioned by Miltitz;
	4–14 July, Leipzig Debate with Eck;

	Charles V, Holy Roman Emperor;
	Swiss Reform Movement begins under Zwingli
1520	15 June, Papal Bull, *Exsurge Domini*;
	August, Luther publishes "Address to German Nobility"
	October, "The Babylonian Captivity of the Church";
	10 October, Papal Bull, *Exsurge Domini*;
	Luther publishes "Freedom of a Christian Man";
	25 November, Luther invited to Diet of Worms;
	10 December, Luther burns Catholic books, and Papal Bull
1521	3 January, Luther excommunicated;
	Justus Jonas, priest, marries;
	16 April, Luther at Worms, "Here I stand . . .";
	Imperial Edict of Worms outlaws Luther;
	4 May, Luther "kidnapped" to Wartburg for safe keeping;
	Corresponds with friends, translates New Testament;
	Henry VIII writes anti-Luther tract and is named
	"Defender of the Faith" by the Pope;
	December, Luther to Wittenberg, one day, to halt reforms
1522	1 March, Luther returns to Wittenberg to lead Reformation;
	September, German New Testament published;
	Diet of Nuremberg, "On Civil Government" and
	"On the Order of Worship" published
1523	Luther's first hymn published (in re: Brussels martyrs)
1524	First hymn book published;
	Peasants War begins;
	Zwingli abolishes the Mass;
	Erasmus publishes "On the Freedom of the Will,"
	opposing Luther
1525	Luther writes against the peasants, condemning
	them, along with radical Reformers;
	5 May, Death of Frederick the Wise, Elector;
	Peasants crushed
	June, marriage to Katherine von Bora;
	December, "The Bondage of the Will" answers Erasmus;
	Elector John succeeds Frederick
1526	May, League of Torgau;
	June, son, Hans, born;
	First Diet of Speyer
1527	"A Mighty Fortress Is Our God";
	Luther's first severe illness;
	Reforms in Hesse and Sweden;
	December, daughter, Elizabeth, born; dies, June, 1528

1529	Catechisms published;
	April, second Diet of Speyer, "Protestants" walk out
1–4 October	Marburg Colloquy, with Swiss Reformers;
	Daughter, Magdalene, born in May;
	Turks besiege Vienna
1530	Diet of Augsburg, Luther at Coburg Castle;
	Smalkaldic League formed by Philip of Hesse
1531	Death of Zwingli, Swiss Reform leader;
	November, son, Martin, born
1532	John Frederick succeeds Elector John
1533	January, son, Paul, born
1534	Publication of German Bible;
	Ingatius Loyola founds Jesuits, counter-reformation
	December, daughter, Margaret, born
1535	Luther refuses commitment to General Council
1536	"Wittenberg Accord" with Swiss and South Germans;
	Outbreak of Anabaptists at Münster
1537	Smalkald Articles by Luther;
	Bugenhagen carries reform to Denmark
1541	Calvin's reforms in Geneva;
	Knox in Scotland
1543	Three tracts "Against the Jews";
	Luther's "Commentary on Genesis";
	Deaths of Copernicus and Holbein
1545	"Against the Papacy," very vitriolic
1545–1563	Council of Trent
1546–1547	Smalkaldic War; Emperor invades Saxony
1546	18 February, death of Luther, at Eisleben
1547	Henry VIII dies

Bibliography

Aland, Kurt. *Four Reformers*. Minneapolis: Augsburg Publishing House, 1979.

Althaus, Paul. (Schultz, Robert C., trans.) *The Theology of Martin Luther*. Philadelpia, Fortress Press, 1966.

Atkinson, James. *Luther: Early Theological Works*. Philadelphia: The Westminster Press, 1962.

Atkinson, James. *Martin Luther and the Birth of Protestantism*. Harmondsworth: Penguin, 1968.

Bainton, Ronald M. *Here I Stand*. New York and Nashville: Abingdon-Cokesbury Press, 1950.

Bainton, Ronald M. *The Reformation of the Sixteenth Century*. Boston: The Beacon Press, 1952.

Bainton, Ronald M. *Women of the Reformation in Germany and Italy*. Minneapolis: Augsburg Publishing House, 1971.

Bevan, Edwin. *Christianity*. London: Oxford University Press, 1948.

Boehmber Heinrich. *Martin Luther: Road to Reformation*. Philadelphia: Round Table Press, 1946.

Booth, E. P. *Martin Luther, Oak of Saxony*. New York: Round Table Press, 1933.

Cambridge Modern History, vol. II—The Reformation. New York: MacMillan, 1934.

Chadwick, Owen. *The Reformation*. Baltimore: Penguin Books, 1964.

Cowie, Leonard. *The Reformation of the Sixteenth Century*. New York: Putnam, 1964.

D'Aubigné, J. H. Merle. *History of the Reformation of the Sixteenth Century*. London: Ward Lock and Co., 1835.

Dickens, A. G. *Martin Luther and the Reformation*. London: Hodder and Stoughton, 1967.

Dickens, A. G. *Reformation and Society in Sixteenth Century Europe*. London: Thames and Hudson, 1966.

Dillenberger, John, ed. *Martin Luther*. Garden City, New York: Doubleday and Company, 1961.

Dimert, Michael. "Points of Origin." *Smithsonian*, November 1983.

Dryer, George H. *History of the Christian Church, vol. 3*. New York, Eaton and Mains, 1903.

Durant, Will. *The Refomation*. New York: Simon and Schuster, 1957.

Ebon, Martin, trans. *Chronicle of Luther's Last Days*. Garden City, New York: Doubleday, 1970.

Bibliography

Eckermann, C. V. *Mistress of the Black Cloister*. Adelaide: Lutheran Publishing House, 1976.

Erickson, Erik. *Young Man Luther*. New York: W.W. Norton and Co., Inc., 1958.

Fisher, George P. *The Reformation*. New York: Chas. Scribner's Sons, 1890.

Fosdick. H. E. *Martin Luther*. New York: Random House, 1956.

Grimm, Harold. *The Reformation Era 1500–1650*. New York: MacMillan, 1973.

Grisar, H. *Martin Luther, His Life and Work*. St Louis, MO, London: B. Herder Book Co., 1930.

Haile, H. G. *Luther—An Experiment in Biography*. Garden City, NY: Doubleday, 1980.

Harbison, E. H. *The Age of Reformation*. Ithaca: Cornell University Press, 1955.

Harbison, E. H. *The Christian Scholar in the Age of Reformation*. New York: Chas. Scribner's Sons, 1956.

Hillerbrand, Hans J., ed. *The Reformation*. New York: Harper and Row, 1964.

Holborn, Hajo. *Ulrich von Hutten and the German Reformation*. New York: Harper and Row, 1937.

Hudson, W. S. *The Story of the Christian Church*. New York: Harper and Brothers, 1958.

Huizinga, Johann. *Erasmus and the Age of Reformation*. New York: Harper and Brothers, 1957.

Hurst, J. *Short History of the Reformation*. New York: Harper and Brothers, 1884.

Johnson, Paul. *A History of Christianity*. New York: Athenium, 1976.

Keppler, Thoms S., ed. *The Fellowship of the Saints*. New York, Nashville: Abingdon-Cokesbury Press, 1948.

Kerr, H. T., ed., *A Compend of Luther's Theology*. Philadelphia, Westminster Press, 1943.

Koestlin, Julius. *Life of Luther*. New York: C. Scribner's Sons, 1883.

Lindsay, Thomas M. *A History of the Reformation*. New York: Charles Scribner's Sons, 1914.

Luther, Martin (Jacobs, C. M., trans.). *Luther's Ninety-Five Theses*. Philadelphia: Fortress Press, 1957.

MacKinnon, James. *Luther and the Reformation*. London, New York, etc.: Longman, Green, and Co., 1930.

Manus, Peter. *Martin Luther.* New York: Crossroad Publishing Co., 1983.

McGiffert, A. C. *Protestant Thought Before Kant*. New York, Chas. Scribner's Sons, 1911.

McManners, John, ed. *The Oxford Illustrated History of Christianity*. New York: Oxford Univerty Press, 1990.

McNeill, John T. *Makers of the Christian Tradition*. New York: Harper and Row, 1964.

Manschreck, Clyde. *Melanchthon: The Quiet Reformer*. Westport, Conn.: Greenwood Press, 1958.

Marty, Martin. *A Short History of Christianity*. New York: Meridian Books, 1959.

Murray, R. H. *Erasmus and Luther*. London: Society for Promoting Christian Knowledge, 1920.

Pelikan, Jaroslev, ed. *Luther's Works—Luther the Expositor*. St. Louis: Concordia Publishing House, 1959.

Rupp, E. G. and Drewery, Benjamin. *Martin Luther*. London: Edward Arnold, 1970.

Rupp, E. G. and Watson, Philipp. *Luther and Erasmus: Free Will and Salvation*. Philadelphia: Westminster Press, 1969.

Seebohm, F. *The Era of the Protestant Revolution*. New York: Chas. Scribner's Sons, 1899.

Simon, Edith. *Luther Alive*. Garden City, New York: Doubleday and Company, 1968.

Smith, Preserved, and Jacobs, C. M., *The Life and Letters of Martin Luther*. Boston and New York: Houghton Mifflin Co., 1911.

Smith, Preserved. *Erasmus*. New York: Dover Publications, 1962.

Sohm, Rudolf. *Outlines of Church History*. Boston: Beacon Press, 1958.

Spitz, Lewis, ed. *The Protestant Reformation*. Englewood Cliffs, New Jersey: Prentice Hall, 1966.

Spitz, Lewis, ed. *The Reformation*, 2nd ed. Lexington: Heath, 1972.

Stepanek, Sally. *Martin Luther*. New York, New Haven, Philadelphia: Chelsea House, 1966.

Tappert, T.G., ed. *Luther: Letters of Spiritual Counsel*. Philadelphia: The Westminster Press, 1955.

Thulin, Oskar, ed. (Deitrick, Martin, trans.). *A Life of Luther*. Philadelphia: Fortress Press, 1966.

Tillmanns, Walter. *The World and Men Around Luther*. Minneapolis: Augsburg Publishing House, 1959.

Todd, John M. *Luther, A Life*. New York, Crossroad, 1982

Vedder, Henry C. *The Reformation in Germany*. New York: The Macmillan Co., 1914.

Walker, Williston. *A History of the Christian Church*. New York, Scribner, 1957.

Whale, J. S. *The Protestant Tradition*. Cambridge: The University Press, 1960.

Winter, Ernst F. ed. *Erasmus and Luther—Discourse on Free Will*. New York: Frederick Morgan Pubishing Co. Inc., 1961.

Index

253